Longman Study Texts

Educating Rita

Longman Study Texts

General editor: Richard Adams

Titles in the series:

Willy Russell

Educating Rita

edited by
Richard Adams

with a personal essay by
Willy Russell

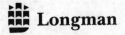 **Longman**

LONGMAN GROUP UK LIMITED
Longman House
Burnt Mill, Harlow, Essex, CM20 2JE, England
and Associated Companies throughout the world.

ISBN 0 582 33182 X

First published 1985
Fourth impression 1987

Set in 10/12pt Linotron 202 Baskerville

Produced by Longman Group (FE) Ltd
Printed in Hong Kong

Contents

Contents

A personal essay

by Willy Russell

Educating the author

I was born in Whiston, which is just outside Liverpool. They
talk funny in Whiston. To a Liverpudlian everyone else talks
funny. Fortunately, when I was five my mum and dad moved
to Knowsley, onto an estate full of Liverpudlians who taught
me how to talk correctly.

My dad worked in a factory (later, having come to hate
factory life, he got out and bought a chip shop) and my mother
worked in a warehouse; in those days there was a common
ritual called employment. I went to school just down the road
from my grandma's mobile grocer's (it was in an old chara-
banc which had long since lost any chance of going anywhere
but everyone called it the mobile).

In school I learned how to read very early. Apart from
reading books I played football and kick-the-can and quite
enjoyed the twice-weekly gardening lessons. We each had a
plot and at the end of the summer term we could take home
our turnips and lettuces and radish and stuff. We used to eat
it on the way. Our headmaster (Pop Chandler) had a war
wound in his leg and everyone said it was 'cause of the
shrapnel. When we went to the baths (if he was in a good
mood) he'd show us this hole in his leg. It was horrible. It was
blue. We loved looking at it.

Other than reading books, gardening, playing football and
looking at shrapnel wounds I didn't care much for school. I
watched the telly a lot. Never went to any theatres or anything
like that. Saw a show at the village hall once but it was all
false. They talked funny and got married at the end. I only
remember it 'cause I won the raffle, a box of fruit, with a

coconut right in the middle. When we opened it the coconut stunk. It was bad.

When I was eleven they sent me to a secondary school in Huyton. Like all the other Knowsley kids I was frightened of Huyton. There were millions of new houses there and flats, and everyone said there were gangs with bike chains and broken bottles and truck spanners. What everyone said was right; playtime was nothing to do with play, it was about survival. Thugs roamed the concrete and casually destroyed anything that couldn't move fast enough. Dinner time was the same only four times as long.

If you were lucky enough to survive the food itself you then had to get out into the playground world of protection rackets, tobacco hustlers, trainee contract killers and plain no-nonsense sadists. And that's without the teachers!

Anders his name was, the metalwork teacher. All the other kids loved metalwork. First thing we had to do was file a small rectangle of metal so that all the sides were straight; this would then be name-stamped and used as a nameplate to identify each kid's work. I never completed mine. After a matter of weeks other kids had moved from making nameplates to producing anything from guns and daggers to boiler-room engines while it was obvious that I was never going to be able to get the sides of my piece of metal straight. Eventually it was just a sliver, a near-perfect needle, though not straight. I showed it to him, Anders; I couldn't hide if from him any longer. He chucked it in the bin and wordlessly handed me another chunk of metal and indicated that I had to do it again and again and again until I did it *right!* And I did, for a whole school year, every metalwork lesson, tried and failed and with every failure there came a chunk of metal and the instruction to do it again. I started to have terrible nightmares about Anders. It's the only time I can remember feeling real hatred for another human being.

After another year I moved schools, to Rainford where it used to be countryside, where they all talked funny, where the thugs were rather old-fashioned, charming even. Whereas in Huyton you could be bike-chained to bits without warning, in Rainford the thugs observed some sort of manners: 'Ey you, does t' want t' fight wi me?' You could still get hurt, of course, and some of the teachers were headcases; but there were no sadists, metalwork was not on the curriculum, there were fields and lawns in place of concrete playgrounds and compared to Huyton it was paradise. We even had a long lesson every week called 'silent reading'; just enter the classroom and pick up a book, start reading and as long as you made no noise you were left completely alone with your book. I remember clearly, during one of these lessons, locked into a novel, the sun streaming through the windows, experiencing the feeling of total peace and security and thinking what a great thing it must be to write books and create in people the sort of feeling the author had created in me. I wanted to be a writer!

It was a wonderful and terrible thought—wonderful because I sensed, I knew, it was the only thing for me. Terrible because how could I, a kid from the 'D' stream, a piece of factory fodder, ever change the course that my life was already set upon? How the hell could I ever be the sort of person who could become a writer? It was a shocking and ludicrous thought, one that I hid deep in myself for years, but one that would not go away.

During my last year at school they took us to a bottle-making factory in St Helens, me and all the other kids who were obviously factory types. I could feel the brutality of the place even before I entered its windowless walls. Inside, the din and the smell were overpowering. Human beings worked in there but the figures I saw, feeding huge and relentlessly hungry machines, seemed not to be a part of humanity but a part of the machinery itself. Those men who were fortunate enough to not have to work directly with the machinery, the supervisors, foremen I suppose, glared, prodded, occasionally shouted. Each one of them looked like Anders from the metal-work class.

Most of the kids with whom I visited that place accepted that it was their lot to end up in that place. Some even talked of the money they would earn and made out that they couldn't wait to get inside those walls.

But, in truth, I think they all dreaded it as much as I. Back in school I stared at the geography books I hadn't read, the history pages and science I hadn't studied, the maths books (which would still be a mystery today, even if I'd studied them from birth), and I realized that with only six months' schooling to go, I'd left it all hopelessly too late. Like it or not I'd end up in a factory. There was no point in trying to catch up with years of schoolwork in a mere six months. And so I didn't. The months I had left were spent sagging school and going to a dark underground club every lunchtime. It was called the Cavern and the smell of sweat in there was as pungent as any in a factory, the din was louder than any made by machines. But the sweat was mingled with cheap perfume and was produced by dancing and the noise was music, made by a group called the Beatles.

One afternoon in summer I left the Cavern after the lunch-time session and had to go to the Bluecoat Chambers to sit an examination, the result of which would determine how suited I was to become an apprentice printer. I didn't want to be an apprentice printer; I wanted to be back in the Cavern. I did the exam because my dad thought it would be a good thing. I answered the questions on how many men it would take to lift three tons of coal in seven hours if it took one man two minutes to lift a sack of coal on a rainy day etc. And I wrote the essay of my choice (titled 'A Group Called The Beatles'). And I failed.

At home there were conferences, discussions, rows and slanging matches all on the same subject—me and the job I'd get. Eventually my mother resolved it all. She suggested I become a ladies' hairdresser! I can only think that a desire to have her hair done free must have clouded her normally reasonable mind. It was such a bizzare suggestion that I went along with it. I went to a college for a year or so and pretended to learn all about hairdressing. In reality most of my time was spent at parties or arranging parties. It was a good year but when it ended I had to go to work. Someone was actually prepared to hire me as a hairdresser, to let me loose on the heads of innocent and unsuspecting customers. There were heads scalded during shampooing, heads which should have become blonde but turned out green, heads of Afro frizz (before Afro frizz had been invented) and heads rendered temporarily bald. Somehow, probably from moving from one shop to another before my legendary abilities were known, I survived. For six years I did a job I didn't understand and didn't like. Eventually I even had my own small salon and it was there that on slack days I would retire to the back room and try to do the one and only thing I felt I understood, felt that I could do: write.

I wrote songs mostly but tried, as well, to write sketches and poetry, even a book. But I kept getting interrupted by women who, reasonably enough on their part, wanted their hair done. It dawned upon me that if ever I was to become a writer I had first to get myself into the sort of world which allowed for, possibly even encouraged such aspiration. But that would mean a drastic change of course. Could I do it? Could I do something which those around me didn't understand? I would have to break away. People would be puzzled and hurt. I compromised. I sensed that the world in which I would be able to write would be the academic world. Students have long holidays. I'd be able to spend a good part of the year writing and the other part learning to do a job, teaching perhaps, which would pay the rent. I wasn't qualified to train as a teacher but I decided to dip my toe in the water and test the temperature. I enrolled in a night class for O level English Literature and passed it. To go to a college though, I'd need at least five O levels. Taking them at night school would take too long. I had to find a college which would let me take a full-time course, pack everything into one year. I found a college but no authority was prepared to give me a maintenance grant or even pay my fees. I knew I couldn't let the course go, knew I could survive from day to day—but how was I going to find the money to pay the fees? The hairdressing paid nothing worth talking of.

I heard of a job, a contract job in Fords, cleaning oil from the girders high above the machinery. With no safety equipment whatsoever and with oil on every girder the danger was obvious. But the money was big.

I packed up the hairdresser's and joined the night-shift girder cleaners. Some of them fell and were injured, some of them took one look at the job and walked away. Eventually there were just a few of us desperate or daft enough to take a chance.

I stayed in that factory just long enough to earn the fees I needed; no extras, nothing. Once I'd earned enough for the fees, I came down from the girders, collected my money and walked away. I enrolled at the college and one day in September made my way along the stone-walled drive. The obvious difference in age between me and the sixteen-year-olds pouring down the drive made me feel exposed and nervous but as I entered the glass doors of Childwall College I felt as if I'd made it back to the beginning. I could start again. I felt at home.

Introduction

First-rate theatre

Since its first appearance (in a Royal Shakespeare Company production) on 10 June 1980, *Educating Rita* has become a firm favourite with British audiences. As well as enjoying a very successful run in London's West End, it has been performed by professional and amateur companies alike up and down the country. It was voted 'Best Comedy of the Year' in 1980. In 1983, it was rated the fourth most popular play on the British stage—and the list included Shakespeare!—while the film version released in the same year was greeted with universal critical acclaim.

Many plays over the years have enjoyed similar meteoric popularity when first staged, only to burn themselves out and fade into obscurity within a relatively short period of time. There are good reasons, however, for supposing that *Educating Rita* will not share such a fate.

To begin with, it is first-rate theatre. In the introduction he wrote recently for a German edition of the play, Willy Russell asserts that for him—as it must be for all working playwrights —the true medium is the *performance*, the book being no more than a record of the text. Certainly, it is on the stage that *Educating Rita* comes fully into its own: if you have not yet seen it performed, then you ought to make a point of doing so as soon as possible. Better still, you might prepare your own workshop production—the play's demands in terms of cast and setting are after all unbelievably modest—and learn for yourself how readily it comes to life in performance. It is a play full of nuance and undertone—misunderstandings, awkwardnesses, double meanings—things that cannot be conveyed anywhere near as successfully on the printed page as they can in a player's facial expression or tone of voice, by a cough, a glance or a shrug. Take, for instance, the following passage from the opening scene: we can certainly detect in general terms the tension between the two characters from a reading of the text—Rita's blunt, direct questioning contrasts amusingly with Frank's embarrassed reluctance to give direct answers. But only in a performance can we appreciate the truth to life of their conversation—only by *seeing* Frank's discomfort and by *hearing* his hesitations:

RITA   (*coming back to the desk*) D' y' get a lot like me?

FRANK   Pardon?

RITA   Do you get a lot of students like me?

FRANK   Not exactly, no . . .

RITA   I was dead surprised when they took me. I don't suppose they would have done if it'd been a proper university. The Open University's different though, isn't it?

FRANK   I've—erm—not had much more experience of it than you. This is the first O.U. work I've done.

RITA   D' y' need the money?

FRANK   I do as a matter of fact.

RITA   It's terrible these days, the money, isn't it? With the inflation an' that. You work for the ordinary university, don't y'? With the real students. The Open University's different, isn't it?

FRANK   It's supposed to embrace a more comprehensive studentship, yes.

RITA   (*inspecting a bookcase*) Degrees for dishwashers.

FRANK   Would you—erm—would you like to sit down?

(pages 3–4)

Variety of appeal

One of the great and most obvious attractions of *Educating Rita* is its humour, ranging from the wryly witty to the downright coarse. It is a humour which springs as much from the relationship of the characters—the clash of two very different cultures and backgrounds—as from the language they speak:

RITA *flounces into the room and goes to the desk.*

RITA   God, I've had enough of this. It's borin', that's what it is, bloody borin'. This Forster, honest to God he doesn't half get on my tits ...

FRANK   Good. You must show me the evidence.

RITA   Y' dirty sod.

FRANK   (*wagging his finger at her*) True, true ... it's cutting down on the booze that's done it.

(page 24)

What is it that amuses us in this exchange? Rita's ripe language, yes, but also the dry allusiveness and detachment of Frank's reaction to it.

But the humour is by no means all. Underneath the teasing, the comic misapprehensions and the repartee, we witness in *Educating Rita* the development of a deep and touching relationship. Willy Russell is quite explicit about his intentions: 'when making *Educating Rita*,' he writes, 'I tried very hard to write a love story.' And it is a love story in the classic mould. In present-day terms, the gulf which separates the two lovers—that of differences in education and social class—is as formidable as that which confronts Romeo and Juliet. But, unlike Shakespeare's play, *Educating Rita*, as we have already seen, is also a comedy: it ends, despite the succession of set-backs that Rita and Frank encounter, in warmth and understanding and good humour.

Commentators have been quick to see parallels between this and other love stories. Some draw attention to the similarity between the education of Rita and that of Eliza Doolittle in Bernard Shaw's *Pygmalion*, as well as the similarity between the relationship of the two pupils with their respective teachers. Willy Russell once found himself arguing in a radio interview with a critic who insisted that the cutting of Frank's hair at the end of the play symbolizes the removal of his power and authority, rather along the lines of the story of Samson and Delilah in the Bible. Although the author denied the validity of this interpretation ('I had merely chosen to end the play with a comic moment, a joke, a gag'), the fact that the critic felt impelled to suggest it reminds us that *Educating Rita* is a play which works in a variety of ways, that makes us think as well as smile.

Thinking as well as smiling

Educating Rita is a play about a twenty-six-year-old Liverpudlian hairdresser who longs for freedom from the dreariness of her daily routine and thinks she can gain it by studying for a degree in English Literature from the Open University. In the course of her education, she teaches her tutor as much about life as she learns from him about books. And she discovers that education can create as many problems as it solves. It is a play which raises a number of important questions and demands that we give them serious and adequate consideration. The section of study questions at the back of this book highlights some of these.

We must beware, however, of misusing the play, of subordinating the whole to a collection of its parts. We must never forget the story in our enthusiasm for some of the issues it raises. To do so would be tantamount to falling into the trap that Rita herself warns us about:

> We was out with the teacher once, y' know outside school, an' I'm right at the back with these other kids an' I saw this fantastic bird, all coloured it was, like dead out of place round our way. I was just gonna shout an' tell Miss but this kid next to me said, 'Keep your mouth shut or she'll make us write an essay on it.'
>
> (page 22)

And Willy Russell himself puts the matter into perspective for us when he writes:

Even though *Educating Rita* is in part about literature, education and language, I wanted to make a play which engaged and was relevant to those who had no knowledge of literature, those who considered themselves uneducated, those whose daily language is not the language of the university or the theatre. In short I wanted to write a play which would attract and be as valid for the Ritas in the audience as the Franks.

That he has been entirely successful in his aim can be judged by the play's wide and growing popularity.

Structure and characterization

In writing *Educating Rita* as what is known in acting circles as a 'two-hander'—that is, a play whose cast consists of just two characters—Willy Russell was setting himself a considerable technical problem. How do you prevent what is essentially an extended though interrupted conversation—conducted, what is more, in one place, without change of scenery—from becoming boring? The answer lies in the great subtlety with which the author has presented his characters and shaded the different stages of the relationship between them.

At the play's opening, we are confronted with a stark contrast: on the one hand, Frank, reserved and cautious in what he says, apologetic about his lack of experience in teaching for the Open University, resentful about having to do so at all; on the other, Rita, exploding on to the stage, prowling about her tutor's room, taking stock of things, making herself at home, dominating the coversation to the point of rudeness.

RITA (*noticing the picture*) That's a nice picture, isn't it? (*She goes up to it*)

FRANK Erm – yes, I suppose it is – nice...

RITA (*studying the picture*) It's very erotic.

FRANK (*looking up*) Actually I don't think I've looked at it for about ten years, but yes, I suppose it is.

RITA There's no suppose about it. Look at those tits.

He coughs and goes back to looking for the admission paper. Is it supposed to be erotic? I mean when he painted it do y' think he wanted to turn people on?

FRANK Erm – probably.

RITA I'll bet he did y' know. Y' don't paint pictures like that just so that people can admire the brush strokes, do y'?

FRANK (*giving a short laugh*) No—no—you're probably right.

RITA This was the pornography of its day, wasn't it? It's sort of like *Men Only*, isn't it? But in those days they had to pretend it wasn't erotic so they made it religious, didn't they? Do *you* think it's erotic?

FRANK (*taking a look*) I think it's very beautiful.

RITA I didn't ask y' if it was beautiful.

(page 3)

This is role reversal with a vengeance: Rita *ought* to be polite, nervous, a little lost in this brave new world of culture. But she is not. Frank *ought* to be confident, sure of his own judgements, direct and clear in his manner of voicing them. But he is the opposite. Indeed, it is *he* who is polite, nervous, lost; *she* who is confident and self-assured.

The development of their relationship from this unusual beginning, and the twists it undergoes in the course of the play, are the things that hold the audience's attention throughout. Why does Rita speak and behave as she does? By the end of the first scene, it is clear that her brashness and swearing are symptoms of a deep-seated unease. By the same point in the play, there is also considerable doubt as to whether she will gain the education for which she craves, her tutor choosing this moment to wax lyrical on the subject of his own inadequacies:

I'm actually an appalling teacher... Most of the time, you see, it doesn't actually matter—appalling teaching is quite in order for most of my appalling students. And the others manage to get by despite me. But you're different. You want a lot, and I can't give it... Everything I know—and you must listen to this—is that I know absolutely nothing.

(page 13)

In the second scene, Frank begins to hold his own in the dialogue more convincingly: discussing literature and education he is on reasonably safe ground. But as soon as the conversation shifts to other topics—life, society, marriage—Rita regains the upper hand. Marriage is, of course, something they have in common; but whereas first his marriage and now his affair with Julia have failed because of Frank's sloth and inadequacy, Rita's relationship with Denny breaks down because she actually encourages it to. Confronted with the choice between marriage and education, she goes for education.

It is scarcely surprising, therefore, that the relationship Rita shares with her teacher should remain decidedly non-sexual. Literature is, after all, her sex-substitute; she has rejected babies in favour of books. Nevertheless, as time passes, it is apparent that what started as a purely professional relationship is becoming emotionally charged—even if Rita herself does not fully appreciate the fact:

FRANK   Perhaps, perhaps your husband thinks you're having an affair with me.

RITA   Oh go way. You're me teacher. I've told him.

FRANK   You've told him about me? What?

RITA   (sitting down) I've—tch—I've tried to explain to him how you give me room to breathe. Y' just, like feed me without expectin' anythin' in return.

(page 33)

Frank responds to Rita's dedication to her studies and her ideal of education by making his own sacrifices: he tries to cut down his drinking, he forgets his dislike of the theatre and accompanies her to an amateur production of *The Importance of Being Earnest*. Later, his affection takes the more conventional form of inviting her to lunch and then to his house for dinner. In next to no time, he is hopelessly dependent upon her: he phones her salon when she fails to turn up for a tutorial; he is jealous of her growing intellectual command, of her freedom to hold meaningful conversations with other students, of her even dreaming of going off to the South of France with them. Bitterly, he equates himself with Frankenstein, whose creature, having been given life, grew beyond the control of its maker. As if to underline how much intellectual independence Rita has gained by Act Two scene three, Willy Russell has her repeating to Frank the very lessons he was teaching her at the beginning of the play. It is now his turn to be narrow and naïve in his judgements; and Rita's to try to educate him to a truer perspective:

RITA ...you're still treating me as though I'm hung up on *Rubyfruit Jungle*... Just... You understand, don't you Frank?

FRANK Entirely, my dear.

RITA I'm sorry.

FRANK Not at all. (*After a pause*) I got around to reading it you know, *Rubyfruit Jungle*. It's excellent.

RITA(*laughing*) Oh go way, Frank. Of its type it's quite interesting. But it's hardly excellence.

(page 63)

The final scene of the play is in some ways ambiguous: we are not really certain how the relationship will develop. Frank acknowledges and accepts the completion of Rita's education and marks the occasion by giving her a dress; Rita, in return, chooses from all the gifts at her disposal as a 'complete' woman to give Frank the one that she had when she first came to him—a haircut. Willy Russell sends us out of the theatre with a smile on our lips, but—tantalizingly—an unsureness in our hearts.

Educating Rita

Characters

FRANK
RITA

Stage directions key:

L	=	LEFT
C	=	CENTRE
DRC	=	DOWN RIGHT CENTRE
UR	=	UP RIGHT
DR	=	DOWN RIGHT
UL	=	UP LEFT
U	=	UP
URC	=	UP RIGHT CENTRE
RC	=	RIGHT CENTRE
R	=	RIGHT

Act One

Scene one

A room on the first floor of a Victorian-built university in the north of England

There is a large bay window L *with a desk placed in front of it and another desk* C *covered with various papers and books. The walls are lined with books and on one wall hangs a good print of a nude religious scene*

When the curtain rises FRANK, *who is in his early fifties, is standing* DRC *holding an empty mug. He goes to the bookcases* DR *and starts taking books from the shelves, hurriedly replacing them before moving on to another section*

FRANK (*looking along the shelves*) Where the hell ...? Eliot? (*He pulls out some books and looks into the bookshelf*) No. (*He replaces the books*) 'E' (*He thinks for a moment*) 'E', 'e' 'e' ... (*Suddenly he remembers*) Dickens. (*Jubilantly he moves to the Dickens section and pulls out a pile of books to reveal a bottle of whisky. He takes the bottle from the shelf and goes to the small table by the door and pours himself a large slug into the mug in his hand*)

The telephone rings and startles him slightly. He manages a gulp at the whisky before he picks up the receiver and although his speech is not slurred, we should recognize the voice of a man who shifts a lot of booze

Yes? ... Of course I'm still here. ... Because I've got this Open University woman coming, haven't I? ... Tch. ... Of course I told you. ... But darling, you shouldn't have prepared dinner should you? Because I said, I distinctly remember saying that I would be late. ... Yes. Yes, I probably shall go to the pub afterwards, I shall need to go to the pub afterwards, I shall need to wash away the

1

memory of some silly woman's attempts to get into the mind of Henry James or whoever it is we're supposed to study on this course. ... Oh God, why did I take this on? ... Yes. ... Yes I suppose I did take it on to pay for the drink. ... Oh, for God's sake, what is it? ... Yes, well— erm—leave it in the oven. ... Look if you're trying to induce some feeling of guilt in me over the prospect of a burnt dinner you should have prepared something other than lamb and ratatouille. ... Because, darling, I like my lamb done to the point of abuse and even I know that ratatouille cannot be burned. ... Darling, you could incinerate ratatouille and still it wouldn't burn. ... What do you mean am I determined to go to the pub? I don't need determination to get me into a pub ...

There is a knock at the door

Look, I'll have to go. ... There's someone at the door. ... Yes, yes I promise. ... Just a couple of pints. ... Four. ...

There is another knock at the door

(*Calling in the direction of the door*) Come in! (*He continues on the telephone*) Yes. ... All right ... yes. ... Bye, bye. ... (*He replaces the receiver*) Yes, that's it, you just pop off and put your head in the oven. (*Shouting*) Come in! Come in!

The door swings open revealing RITA

RITA (*from the doorway*) I'm comin' in, aren't I? It's that stupid bleedin' handle on the door. You wanna get it fixed! (*She comes into the room*)

FRANK (*staring, slightly confused*) Erm—yes, I suppose I always mean to ...

RITA (*going to the chair by the desk and dumping her bag*) Well that's no good always meanin' to, is it? Y' should get on with it; one of these days you'll be shoutin' 'Come in' an' it'll go on forever because the poor sod on the other side won't be able to get in. An' you won't be able to get out.

FRANK *stares at* RITA *who stands by the desk*

FRANK You are?

RITA   What am I?

FRANK   Pardon?

RITA   What?

FRANK   (*looking for the admission papers*) Now you are?

RITA   I'm a what?

FRANK *looks up and then returns to the papers as* RITA *goes to hang her coat on the door hooks*

RITA   (*noticing the picture*) That's a nice picture, isn't is? (*She goes up to it*)

FRANK   Erm—yes, I suppose it is—nice …

RITA   (*studying the picture*) It's very erotic.

FRANK   (*looking up*) Actually I don't think I've looked at it for about ten years, but yes, I suppose it is.

RITA   There's no suppose about it. Look at those tits.

He coughs and goes back to looking for the admission paper

   Is it supposed to be erotic? I mean when he painted it do y' think he wanted to turn people on?

FRANK   Erm—probably.

RITA   I'll bet he did y' know. Y' don't paint pictures like that just so that people can admire the brush strokes, do y'?

FRANK   (*giving a short laugh*) No—no—you're probably right.

RITA   This was the pornography of its day, wasn't it? It's sort of like *Men Only*, isn't it? But in those days they had to pretend it wasn't erotic so they made it religious, didn't they? Do *you* think it's erotic?

FRANK   (*taking a look*) I think it's very beautiful.

RITA   I didn't ask y' if it was beautiful.

FRANK   But the term 'beautiful' covers the many feelings I have about that picture, including the feeling that, yes, it is erotic.

RITA   (*coming back to the desk*) D' y' get a lot like me?

FRANK   Pardon?

RITA   Do you get a lot of students like me?

3

FRANK Not exactly, no ...

RITA I was dead surprised when they took me. I don't suppose they would have done if it'd been a proper university. The Open University's different though, isn't it?

FRANK I've—erm—not had much more experience of it than you. This is the first O. U. work I've done.

RITA D' y' need the money?

FRANK I do as a matter of fact.

RITA It's terrible these days, the money, isn't it? With the inflation an' that. You work for the ordinary university, don't y'? With the real students. The Open University's different, isn't it?

FRANK It's supposed to embrace a more comprehensive studentship, yes.

RITA (inspecting a bookcase) Degrees for dishwashers.

FRANK Would you—erm—would you like to sit down?

RITA No! Can I smoke? (She goes to her bag and rummages in it)

FRANK Tobacco?

RITA Yeh. (She half-laughs) Was that a joke? (She takes out a packet of cigarettes and a lighter) Here—d' y' want one? (She takes out two cigarettes and dumps the packet on the desk)

FRANK (after a pause) Ah—I'd love one.

RITA Well, have one.

FRANK (after a pause) I—don't smoke—I made a promise not to smoke.

RITA Well, I won't tell anyone.

FRANK Promise?

As FRANK goes to take the cigarette RITA whips it from his reach

RITA (doing a Brownie salute) On my oath as an ex Brownie. (She gives him the cigarette) I hate smokin' on me own. An' everyone seems to have packed up these days. (She lights the cigarettes) They're all afraid of gettin' cancer.

FRANK looks dubiously at his cigarette

RITA But they're all cowards.

FRANK Are they?

RITA   You've got to challenge death an' disease. I read this poem about fightin' death ...

FRANK   Ah—Dylan Thomas ...

RITA   No. Roger McGough. It was about this old man who runs away from hospital an' goes out on the ale. He gets pissed an' stands in the street shoutin' an' challengin' death to come out an' fight. It's dead good.

FRANK   Yes. I don't think I know the actual piece you mean ...

RITA   I'll bring y' the book—it's great.

FRANK   Thank you.

RITA   You probably won't think it's any good.

FRANK   Why?

RITA   It's the sort of poetry you can understand.

FRANK   Ah. I see.

RITA *begins looking idly round the room*

FRANK   Can I offer you a drink?

RITA   What of?

FRANK   Scotch?

RITA   (*going to the bookcase* UR) Y' wanna be careful with that stuff, it kills y' brain cells.

FRANK   But you'll have one? (*He gets up and goes to the small table*)

RITA   All right. It'll probably have a job findin' my brain.

FRANK   (*pouring the drinks*) Water?

RITA   (*looking at the bookcase*) Yeh, all right. (*She takes a copy of 'Howards End' from the shelf*) What's this like?

FRANK *goes over to* RITA, *looks at the title of the book and then goes back to the drinks*

FRANK   Howards End?

RITA   Yeh. It sounds filthy, doesn't it? E. M. Foster.

FRANK   Forster.

RITA   Oh yeh. What's it like?

FRANK   Borrow it. Read it.

RITA   Ta. I'll look after it. (*She moves back towards the desk*) If I pack the course in I'll post it to y'.

5

FRANK *comes to the desk with drinks*

FRANK (*handing her the mug*) Pack it in? Why should you do that?

RITA *puts her drink down on the desk and puts the copy of 'Howards End' in her bag*

RITA I just might. I might decide it was a soft idea.

FRANK (*looking at her*) Mm. Cheers. If—erm—if you're already contemplating 'packing it in', why did you enrol in the first place?

RITA Because I wanna know.

FRANK What do you want to know?

RITA Everything.

FRANK Everything? That's rather a lot, isn't it? Where would you like to start?

RITA Well, I'm a student now, aren't I? I'll have to do exams, won't I?

FRANK Yes. Eventually.

RITA I'll have to learn about it all, won' I? Yeh. It's like y' sit there, don't y', watchin' the ballet or the opera on the telly an'—an' y' call it rubbish cos that's what it looks like? Cos y' don't understand. So y' switch it off an' say, that's fuckin' rubbish.

FRANK Do you?

RITA I do. But I don't want to. I wanna see. Y' don't mind me swearin', do y'?

FRANK Not at all.

RITA Do you swear?

FRANK Never stop.

RITA See, the educated classes know it's only words, don't they? It's only the masses who don't understand. I do it to shock them sometimes. Y' know when I'm in the hairdresser's—that's where I work —I'll say somethin' like, 'Oh, I'm really fucked', y' know, dead loud. It doesn't half cause a fuss.

FRANK Yes—I'm sure ...

RITA But it doesn't cause any sort of fuss with educated

people, does it? Cos they know it's only words and they don't worry. But these stuck-up idiots I meet, they think they're royalty just cos they don't swear; an' I wouldn't mind but it's the aristocracy that swears more than anyone, isn't it? They're effin' an' blindin' all day long. It's all 'Pass me the fackin' grouse' with them, isn't is? But y' can't tell them that round our way. It's not their fault; they can't help it. (*She goes to the window and looks out*) But sometimes I hate them. God, what's it like to be free?

FRANK Ah. Now there's a question. Will you have another drink? (*He goes to the small table*)

RITA (*shaking her head*) If I'd got some other tutor I wouldn't have stayed.

FRANK (*pouring himself a drink*) What sort of other tutor?

RITA Y' know, someone who objected to swearin'.

FRANK How did you know I wouldn't object?

RITA I didn't. I was just testin' y'.

FRANK (*coming back to the desk and looking at her*) Yes. You're doing rather a lot of that, aren't you?

RITA That's what I do. Y' know, when I'm nervous.

FRANK (*sitting in the swivel chair*) And how am I scoring so far?

RITA Very good, ten out of ten go to the top of the class an' collect a gold star. I love this room. I love that window. Do you like it?

FRANK What?

RITA The window.

FRANK I don't often consider it actually. I sometimes get an urge to throw something through it.

RITA What?

FRANK A student usually.

RITA (*smiling*) You're bleedin' mad you, aren't y'?

FRANK Probably.

Pause

RITA Aren't you supposed to be interviewin' me?

FRANK (*looking at the drink*) Do I need to?

RITA I talk too much, don't I? I know I talk a lot. I don't at

7

home. I hardly ever talk when I'm there. But I don't often get the chance to talk to someone like you; to talk at you. D' y' mind?

FRANK   Would you be at all bothered if I did?

She shakes her head and then turns it into a nod

I don't mind. (*He takes a sip of his drink*)

RITA   What does assonance mean?

FRANK   (*half-spluttering*) What? (*He gives a short laugh*)

RITA   Don't laugh at me.

FRANK   No. Erm—assonance. Well, it's a form of rhyme. What's a—what's an example—erm—? Do you know Yeats?

RITA   The wine lodge?

FRANK   Yeats the poet.

RITA   No.

FRANK   Oh. Well—there's a Yeats poem, called 'The Wild Swans at Coole'. In it he rhymes the word 'swan' with the word 'stone'. There, you see, an example of assonance.

RITA   Oh. It means gettin' the rhyme wrong.

FRANK   (*looking at her and laughing*) I've never really looked at it like that. But yes, yes you could say it means getting the rhyme wrong; but purposefully, in order to achieve a certain effect.

RITA   Oh. (*There is a pause and she wanders round*) There's loads I don't know.

FRANK   And you want to know everything?

RITA   Yeh.

FRANK *nods and then takes her admission paper from his desk and looks at it*

FRANK   What's your name?

RITA   (*moving towards the bookcase*) Rita.

FRANK   (*looking at the paper*) Rita. Mm. It says here Mrs S. White.

RITA *goes to the right of* FRANK, *takes a pencil, leans over and scratches out the initial 'S'*

RITA   That's 'S' for Susan. It's just me real name. I've

8

changed it to Rita, though. I'm not a Susan anymore. I've called meself Rita—y' know, after Rita Mae Brown.

FRANK   Who?

RITA   Y' know, Rita Mae Brown who wrote *Rubyfruit Jungle?* Haven't y' read it? It's a fantastic book. D' y' wanna lend it?

FRANK   I'd—erm—I'd be very interested.

RITA   All right.

RITA *gets a copy of 'Rubyfruit Jungle' from her bag and gives it to* FRANK. *He turns it over and reads the blurb on the back cover*

What's your name?

FRANK   Frank.

RITA   Oh. Not after Frank Harris?

FRANK   Not after Frank anyone.

RITA   Maybe y' parents named y' after the quality. (*She sits in the chair by the desk*)

FRANK *puts down 'Rubyfruit Jungle'*

RITA   Y' know Frank, Frank Ness, Elliot's brother.

FRANK   What?

RITA   I'm sorry—it was a joke. Y' know, Frank Ness, Elliot's brother.

FRANK   (*bemused*) Ah.

RITA   You've still not got it, have y'? Elliot Ness—y' know, the famous Chicago copper who caught Al Capone.

FRANK   Ah. When you said Elliot I assumed you meant T. S. Eliot.

RITA   Have you read his stuff?

FRANK   Yes.

RITA   All of it?

FRANK   Every last syllable.

RITA   (*impressed*) Honest? I couldn't even get through one poem. I tried to read this thing he wrote called 'J. Arthur Prufrock'; I couldn't finish it.

FRANK   'J. Alfred'.

RITA   What?

FRANK   I think you'll find it was 'J. Alfred Prufrock', Rita. J. Arthur is something else altogether.

RITA   Oh yeh. I never thought of that. I've not half got a lot to learn, haven't I?

FRANK   (*looking at her paper*) You're a ladies' hairdresser?

RITA   Yeh.

FRANK   Are you good at it?

RITA   (*getting up and wandering around*) I am when I wanna be. Most of the time I don't want to though. They get on me nerves.

FRANK   Who?

RITA   The women. They never tell y' things that matter. Like, y' know, doin' a perm, well y' can't use a strong perm lotion on a head that's been bleached with certain sorts of cheap bleach. It makes all the hair break off. But at least once a month I'll get a customer in for a perm who'll swear to God that she's not had any bleach on; an' I can tell, I mean I can see it. So y' go ahead an' do the perm an' she comes out the drier with half an inch of stubble.

FRANK   And what do you do about it?

RITA   Try and sell them a wig.

FRANK   My God.

RITA   Women who want their hair doin', they won't stop at anythin', y' know. Even the pensioners are like that, y' know; a pensioner'll come in an' she won't tell y' that she's got a hearin' aid: so y' start cuttin' don't y'? Next thing—snip—another granny deaf for a fortnight. I'm always cuttin' hearin' aid cords. An' ear lobes.

FRANK   You sound like something of a liability.

RITA   I am. But they expect too much. They walk in the hairdresser's an' an hour later they wanna walk out a different person. I tell them I'm a hairdresser, not a plastic surgeon. It's worse when there's a fad on, y' know like Farrah Fawcett Majors.

FRANK   Who?

RITA Far-rah Fawcett Majors. Y' know, she used to be with
Charlie's Angels.

FRANK *remains blank*

RITA It's a telly programme on ITV.

FRANK Ah.

RITA (*wandering towards the door*) You wouldn't watch ITV
though, would y'? It's all BBC with you, isn't it?

FRANK Well, I must confess ...

RITA It's all right, I know. Soon as I walked in here I said to
meself, 'Y' can tell he's a Flora man'.

FRANK A what?

RITA A Flora man.

FRANK Flora? Flowers?

RITA (*coming back to the desk*) No, Flora, the bleedin' margarine, no cholesterol; it's for people like you who eat pebble-
dashed bread, y' know the bread, with little hard bits in it,
just like pebble-dashin'.

FRANK (*realizing and smiling*) Ah—pebble-dashed bread.

✦ RITA Quick? He's like lightnin'. But these women, you see,
they come to the hairdresser's cos they wanna be changed.
But if you want to change y' have to do it from the inside,
don't y? Know like I'm doin'. Do y' think I'll be able to do
it?

FRANK Well, it really depends on you, on how committed you
are. Are you sure that you're absolutely serious about want-
ing to learn?

RITA I'm dead serious. Look, I know I take the piss
an' that but I'm dead serious really. I take the piss because
I'm not, y' know, confident like, but I wanna be, honest.

*He nods and looks at her. She becomes uncomfortable and moves away a
little*

Tch. What y' lookin' at me for?

FRANK Because—I think you're marvellous. Do you know, I
think you're the first breath of air that's been in this room
for years.

RITA (*wandering around*) Tch. Now who's taking the piss?

11

FRANK   Don't you recognize a compliment?

RITA   Go way ...

FRANK   Where to?

RITA   Don't be soft. Y' know what I mean.

FRANK   What I want to know is what is it that's suddenly led you to this?

RITA   What? Comin' here?

FRANK   Yes.

RITA   It's not sudden.

FRANK   Ah.

RITA   I've been realizin' for ages that I was, y' know, slightly out of step. I'm twenty-six. I should have had a baby by now; everyone expects it. I'm sure me husband thinks I'm sterile. He was moanin' all the time, y' know, 'Come off the pill, let's have a baby'. I told him I'd come off it, just to shut him up. But I'm still on it. (*She moves round to* FRANK) See, I don't wanna baby yet. See, I wanna discover meself first. Do you understand that?

FRANK   Yes.

RITA   (*moving to the chair* U *of the desk and fiddling with it*) Yeh. They wouldn't round our way. They'd think I was mental. I've tried to explain it to me husband but between you an' me I think he's thick. No, he's not thick, he's blind, he doesn't want to see. You know if I'm readin', or watchin' somethin' different on the telly he gets dead narked. I used to just tell him to piss off but then I realized that it was no good doin' that, that I had to explain to him. I tried to explain that I wanted a better way of livin' me life. An' he listened to me. But he didn't understand because when I'd finished he said he agreed with me and that we should start savin' the money to move off our estate an' get a house out in Formby. Even if it was a new house I wanted I wouldn't go an' live in Formby. I hate that hole, don't you?

FRANK   Yes.

RITA   Where do you live?

FRANK   Formby.

RITA (*sitting*) Oh.

FRANK (*getting up and going to the small table*) Another drink?

She shakes her head

You don't mind if I do? (*He pours himself a drink*)

RITA No. It's your brain cells y' killin'.

FRANK (*smiling*) All dead long ago I'm afraid. (*He drinks*)

RITA *gets up and goes to Frank's chair. She plays with the swivel and then leans on it*

RITA When d' y' actually, y' know, start teaching me?

FRANK (*looking at her*) What can I teach you?

RITA Everything.

FRANK *leans on the filing cabinet, drinks, shakes his head and looks at her*

FRANK I'll make a bargain with you. Yes? I'll tell you everything I know—but if I do that you must promise never to
come back here ... You see I never—I didn't actually want
to take this course in the first place. I allowed myself to be
talked into it. I knew it was wrong. Seeing you only confirms
my suspicion. My dear, it's not your fault, just the luck of
the draw that you got me; but get me you did. And the thing
is, between you, me and the walls, I'm actually an appalling
teacher. (*After a pause*) Most of the time, you see, it doesn't
actually matter—appalling teaching is quite in order for
most of my appalling students. And the others manage to get
by despite me. But you're different. You want a lot, and I
can't give it. (*He moves towards her*) Everything I know—and
you must listen to this—is that I know absolutely nothing. I
don't like the hours, you know. (*He goes to the swivel chair and
sits*) Strange hours for this Open University thing. They
expect us to teach when the pubs are open. I can be a good
teacher when I'm in the pub, you know. Four pints of weak
Guinness and I can be as witty as Wilde. I'm sorry—there
are other tutors—I'll arrange it for you ... post it on ... (*He
looks at her*)

RITA *slowly turns and goes towards the door. She goes out and quietly
closes the door behind her. Suddenly the door bursts open and* RITA *flies in*

13

RITA   (*going up to him*) Wait a minute, listen to me. Listen: I'm on this course, you are my teacher—an' you're gonna bleedin' well teach me.

FRANK   There are other tutors—I've told you …

RITA   You're my tutor. I don't want another tutor.

FRANK   For God's sake, woman—I've told you …

RITA   You're my tutor.

FRANK   But I've told you—I don't want to do it. Why come to me?

RITA   (*looking at him*) Because you're a crazy mad piss artist who wants to throw his students through the window, an' I like you. (*After a pause*) Don't you recognize a compliment?

FRANK   Do you think I could have a cigarette?

RITA   (*offering the packet of cigarettes*) I'll bring me scissors next week and give y' a haircut.

FRANK   You're not coming here next week.

RITA   (*lighting his cigarette*) I am. And you're gettin' y' hair cut.

FRANK   I am not getting my hair cut.

RITA   (*getting her bag*) I suppose y' wanna walk round like that, do y'? (*She goes towards the door*)

FRANK   Like what?

RITA   (*getting her coat*) Like a geriatric hippie.

Black out

RITA *exits*

Scene two

The lights come up on FRANK *who is standing in the centre of the room. He glances at his watch, moves to the window, looks out, glances at his watch again and then moves across to the books. He glances at his watch and then his attention is caught by the door handle being turned. He looks at the door but no one enters although the handle keeps being turned. Eventually he goes to the door and pulls it open*

RITA *is standing in the doorway, holding a small can of oil*

FRANK Oh.

RITA Hello. I was just oilin' it for y'. (*She comes into the room*) I knew you wouldn't get round to it. Y' can have that.

She gives the oil can to FRANK

FRANK Erm—thanks. (*He puts the can on the filing cabinet and then goes and sits in the swivel chair*)

Slightly amused, he watches her as she wanders round the room

RITA (*turning to him*) What y' lookin' at?

FRANK Don't you ever just walk into a room and sit down?

RITA Not when I've got the chair with its back to the door.

FRANK (*getting up*) Well—if it'd make you happier you take my chair.

RITA No. You're the teacher, you sit there.

FRANK But it doesn't matter where I sit. If you'd be happier with that chair then you sit there.

RITA Tch. Is that what y' call democracy at work? I don't wanna sit down anyway. I like walkin' around this room. (*After a pause*) How d' y' make a room like this?

FRANK I didn't make it. I just moved in. The rest sort of happened.

RITA (*looking round*) Yeh. That's cos you've got taste. I'm gonna have a room like this one day. There's nothing phoney about it. Everything's in its right place. (*After a pause*) It's a mess. But it's a perfect mess. (*She wanders around*) It's like wherever you've put something down it's grown to fit there.

FRANK (*sitting down*) You mean that over the years it's acquired a certain patina.

RITA Do I?

FRANK I think so.

RITA Yeh. 'It's acquired a certain patina.' It's like somethin' from a romantic film, isn't it? 'Over the years your face has acquired a certain patina.'

FRANK *smiles*

RITA (*sniffing*) You've not been drinking, have y'?

FRANK No.

15

RITA   Is that because of me, because of what I said last week?

FRANK   (*laughing*) My God. You think you've reformed me?

RITA   (*going to the window*) I don't wanna reform y'. Y' can do what y' like. (*Quickly*) I love that lawn down there. When it's summer do they sit on it?

FRANK   (*going to the window*) Who?

RITA   (*going back to the desk*) The ones who come here all the time. The proper students.

FRANK   Yes. First glimmer of sun and they're all out there.

RITA   Readin' an' studyin'?

FRANK   Reading and studying? What do you think they are, human? Proper students don't read and study.

RITA   Y' what?

FRANK   A joke, a joke. Yes. They read and study, sometimes.

Pause. RITA *dumps her bag on the chair and then goes and hangs up her coat on the door*

RITA   It looks the way I always imagined a public school to look, y' know a boardin' school. When I was a kid I always wanted to go to a boardin' school.

FRANK   God forbid it; why?

RITA   (*going to her chair at the desk*) I always thought they sounded great, schools like that, y' know with a tuck-shop an' a matron an' prep. An' a pair of kids called Jones minor an' Jones major. I told me mother once. (*She opens her bag and takes out the copy of 'Howards End', ring bound file, note-pad, ruler and pencil-case, placing them methodically on the desk in front of her*) She said I was off me cake.

FRANK   (*with an exaggerated look at her*) What in the name of God is being off one's cake?

RITA   Soft. Y' know, mental.

FRANK   Aha. I must remember that. The next student to ask me if Isabel Archer was guilty of protestant masochism shall be told that one is obviously very off one's cake!

RITA   Don't be soft. You can't say that.

FRANK   Whyever not?

RITA   You can't. If you do it, it's slummin' it. Comin' from you it'd sound dead affected, wouldn't it?

FRANK   Dead affected?

RITA   Yeh. You say that to your proper students they'll think you're off your—y' know ...

FRANK   Cake, yes. Erm—Rita, why didn't you ever become what you call a proper student?

RITA   What? After goin' to the school I went to?

FRANK   Was it bad?

RITA *starts sharpening the pencils one by one into perfect spikes, leaving the shavings on the desk*

RITA   Nah, just normal, y' know; borin', ripped-up books, broken glass everywhere, knives an' fights. An' that was just in the staffroom. Nah, they tried their best I suppose, always tellin' us we stood more of a chance if we studied. But studyin' was just for the whimps, wasn't it? See, if I'd started takin' school seriously I would have had to become different from me mates, an' that's not allowed.

FRANK   By whom?

RITA   By your mates, by your family, by everyone. So y' never admit that school could be anythin' other than useless.

FRANK *passes her the ashtray but she ignores it and continues sharpening the pencils on to the table*

RITA   Like what you've got to be into is music an' clothes an' lookin' for a feller, y' know the real qualities of life. Not that I went along with it so reluctantly. I mean, there was always somethin' in me head, tappin' away, tellin' me I might have got it all wrong. But I'd just play another record or buy another dress an' stop worryin'. There's always somethin' to make you forget about it. So y' do, y' keep goin', tellin' yourself life's great. There's always another club to go to, a new feller to be chasin', a laugh an' a joke with the girls. Till, one day, y' own up to yourself an' y' say, is this it? Is this the absolute maximum I can expect from this livin' lark? An' that's the big moment that one, that's the point when y'

17

have to decide whether it's gonna be another change of dress or a change in yourself. An' it's really temptin' to go out an' get another dress y' know, it is. Cos it's easy, it doesn't cost anythin', it doesn't upset anyone around y'. Like cos they don't want y' to change.

FRANK But you—erm—you managed to resist another new dress?

RITA Can't y' tell? Look at the state of this; I haven't had a new dress in twelve months. An' I'm not gonna get one either, not till—till I pass me first exam. Then I'll get a proper dress, the sort of dress you'd only see on an educated woman, on the sort of woman who knows the difference between Jane Austen an' Tracy Austin. (*She finishes sharpening the last pencil, and arranges it in line with the others. She gathers the pencil shavings into her hand and chucks them in the waste-bin*) Let's start.

FRANK Now the piece you wrote for me on—what was it called …?

RITA (*getting out her cigarettes and lighter*) Rubyfruit Jungle.

FRANK Yes, it was—erm …

RITA Crap?

FRANK No. Erm—the thing is, it was an appreciation, a descriptive piece. What you have to learn is criticism.

RITA What's the difference? (*She lights a cigarette*)

FRANK Well. You must try to remember that criticism is purely objective. It should be approached almost as a science. It must be supported by reference to established literary critique. Criticism is never subjective and should not be confused with partisan interpretation. In criticism sentiment has no place. (*He picks up the copy of 'Howards End'*) Tell me, what did you think of *Howards End*?

RITA It was crap.

FRANK What?

RITA I thought it was crap!

FRANK Crap? And who are you citing in support of your thesis, F. R. Leavis?

RITA No. Me!

FRANK What have I just said? 'Me' is subjective.

RITA Well it's what I think.

FRANK You think *Howards End* is crap? Well would you kindly tell me why you think it's quote, 'Crap', unquote.

RITA Yeh, I will tell y'. It's crap because the feller who wrote it was a louse. Because halfway through that book I couldn't go on readin' it because he, Mr Bleedin' E. M. Forster says, quote 'We are not concerned with the poor' unquote. That's why it's crap. An' that's why I didn't go on readin' it, that's why.

FRANK (*astounded*) Because he said we are not concerned with the poor?

RITA Yeh, that's it!

FRANK But he wasn't writing about the poor.

RITA When he wrote that book the conditions of the poor in this country were appalling. An' he's sayin' he couldn't care less. Mr E. M. Bleedin' Foster.

FRANK Forster.

RITA I don't care what his name was, he was sittin' up there in his ivory tower an' sayin' he couldn't care less.

FRANK *laughs*

RITA Don't laugh at me.

FRANK (*getting up*) But you cannot interpret E. M. Forster from a Marxist viewpoint.

RITA Why?

FRANK Look, before discussing this I said no subjectivity, no sentimentality.

RITA I wasn't bein' sentimental.

FRANK Of course you were. You stopped reading the book because you wanted Forster to concern himself with the poor. Literature can ignore the poor.

RITA Well, it's immoral.

FRANK (*wandering around*) Amoral. But you wanted to know. You see what sort of a mark you'd get if you approached Forster in this way during an examination?

RITA   What sort?

FRANK   Well, you might manage one or two per cent if the examiner was sympathetic to the one dubious quality your criticism displays.

RITA   What's that?

FRANK   Brevity.

RITA   All right. But I hated that book. Can't we do somethin' else? Can't we do somethin' I like?

FRANK   But the sort of stuff you like is not necessarily the sort of thing that will form the basis of your examination next Christmas. Now if you're going to pass any sort of exam you have to begin to discipline that mind of yours.

RITA   Are you married?

FRANK   (moving back to the swivel chair) It's—ogh ...

RITA   Are y'? What's y' wife like?

FRANK   Is my wife at all relevant?

RITA   What? You should know, you married her.

FRANK   Well, she's not relevant. I haven't seen her for a long time. We split up. All right?

RITA   I'm sorry.

FRANK   Why are you sorry?

RITA   I'm sorry for askin'. For bein' nosey.

FRANK   (sitting in the swivel chair) The thing about Howards End is that ...

RITA   Why did y' split up?

FRANK   (taking off his glasses and looking at her) Perhaps you'd like to take notes! When you have to answer a question on Forster you can treat the examiner to an essay called Frank's marriage!

RITA   Oh go way. I'm only interested.

FRANK   (leaning towards her; conspiratorially) We split up, Rita, because of poetry.

RITA   Y' what?

FRANK   One day my wife pointed out to me that for fifteen years my output as a poet had dealt exclusively with the period in which we—discovered each other.

RITA   Are you a poet?

FRANK   Was. And so, to give me something new to write about she left. A very noble woman my wife. She left me for the good of literature.

RITA   An' what happened?

FRANK   She was right. Her leaving was an enormous benefit to literature.

RITA   What, y' wrote a load of good stuff?

FRANK   No. I stopped writing altogether.

RITA   (*slightly puzzled*) Are you takin' the piss?

FRANK *gives a short laugh and leans back in his chair*

FRANK   No.

RITA   People don't split up because of things like that. Because of literature.

FRANK   Maybe you're right. But that's how I remember it.

RITA   Were you a famous poet?

FRANK   No. I sold a few books, all out of print now.

RITA   Can I read some of your stuff?

FRANK   You wouldn't like it.

RITA   How d' y' know?

FRANK   It's the sort of poetry you can't understand—unless you happen to have a detailed knowledge of the literary references.

RITA   Oh. (*After a pause*) Do you live on y' own then?

FRANK   Rita! Tch.

RITA   I was only askin'.

FRANK   I live with a girl. Ex student. She's very caring, very tolerant, admires me enormously and spends a great deal of time putting her head in the oven.

RITA   Does she try an' do herself in?

FRANK   Mm? No, she just likes to watch the ratatouille cook.

RITA   The what?

FRANK   Ratatouille. Though Julia has renamed it the 'stop-outs dish'. It can simmer in an oven for days. In our house it often has no choice.

RITA   D' you stop out for days?

FRANK   Occasionally. And that is the end of . . .

RITA   Why do y'?

FRANK   And that is the end of that.

RITA   If y' were mine an' y' stopped out for days y' wouldn't get back in.

FRANK   Ah, but Rita, if I was yours would I stop out for days?

RITA   Don't y' like Julia?

FRANK   I like her enormously; it's myself I'm not too fond of.

RITA   Tch. Y' great . . .

FRANK   A vote of confidence; thank you. But, I'm afraid, Rita, that you'll find there's less to me than meets the eye.

RITA   See—look—y' can say dead clever things like that, can't y'? I wish I could talk like that. It's brilliant.

FRANK   Staggering. Now look, *Howards* . . . (*He swivels the chair round so that he faces away from* RITA)

RITA   Oh ey . . . leave that. I just like talkin' to y'. It's great. That's what they do wrong in schools y' know—(*she gets up and warms her legs by the fire*)—they get y' talkin' an' that, an' y' all havin' a great time talkin' about somethin' an' the next thing they wanna do is turn it into a lesson. We was out with the teacher once, y' know outside school, an' I'm right at the back with these other kids an' I saw this fantastic bird, all coloured it was, like dead out of place round our way. I was just gonna shout an' tell Miss but this kid next to me said, 'Keep your mouth shut or she'll make us write an essay on it.'

FRANK   (*sighing*) Yes, that's what we do, Rita; we call it education.

RITA   Tch. Y'd think there was somethin' wrong with education to hear you talk.

FRANK   Perhaps there is.

RITA   So why are y' givin' me an education?

FRANK   Because it's what you want, isn't it? What I'd actually like to do is take you by the hand and run out of this room forever.

RITA   (*going back to her chair*) Tch—be serious . . .

FRANK   I am. Right now there's a thousand things I'd rather do than teach; most of them with you, young lady ...

RITA   (*smiling gently*) Tch. Oh sod off ... You just like saying things like that. (*She sits down*)

FRANK   Do I?

RITA   Yeh. Y' know y' do.

FRANK   Rita—why didn't you walk in here twenty years ago?

RITA   Cos I don't think they would have accepted me at the age of six.

FRANK   You know what I mean.

RITA   I know. But it's not twenty years ago, Frank. It's now. You're there an' I'm here.

FRANK   Yes. And you're here for an education. (*He waves his finger*) You must keep reminding me of that. Come on, Forster!

RITA   Tch. Forget him.

FRANK   Listen to me; you said that I was going to teach you. You want to learn. Well that, I'm afraid, means a lot of work. You've barely had a basic schooling, you've never passed an examination in your life. Possessing a hungry mind is not, in itself, a guarantee of success.

RITA   All right. But I just don't like *Howards* bleedin' *End*.

FRANK   Then go back to what you do like and stop wasting my time. You go out and buy yourself a new dress and I'll go to the pub.

RITA   (*after a pause*) Is that you putting your foot down?

FRANK   It is actually.

RITA   Oh. Aren't you impressive when y' angry?

FRANK   Forster!

RITA   All right, all right, Forster. Does Forster's repeated use of the phrase 'only connect' suggest that he was really a frustrated electrician?

FRANK   Rita.

RITA   In considering Forster it helps if we examine the thirteen amp plug ...

Black-out

RITA *goes out*

23

Scene three

The lights come up on FRANK *working at his desk*

RITA *flounces into the room and goes to the desk*

RITA   God, I've had enough of this. It's borin', that's what it is, bloody borin'. This Forster, honest to God he doesn't half get on my tits.

She dumps her bag on the chair and makes towards the hook by the door, taking off her coat as she goes. She hangs the coat on the hook

FRANK   Good. You must show me the evidence.

RITA   Y' dirty sod.

FRANK   (*Wagging his finger at her*) True, true ... it's cutting down on the booze that's done it. Now. (*He waves a sheet of paper at her*) What's this?

RITA   (*sitting by the desk*) It's a bleedin' piece of paper, isn't it?

FRANK   It's your essay. Is it a joke? Is it?

RITA   No. It's not a joke.

FRANK   Rita, how the hell can you write an essay on E. M. Forster with almost total reference to Harold Robbins?

RITA   Well? You said bring in other authors.

FRANK   Tch.

RITA   Don't go on at me. You said; y' said, 'Reference to other authors will impress the examiners'.

FRANK   I said refer to other works but I don't think the examiner, God bless him, will have read, (*he consults the paper*) *A Stone For Danny Fisher*.

RITA   Well, that's his hard luck, isn't it?

FRANK   It'll be your hard luck when he fails your paper.

RITA   Oh that's prime, isn't it? That's justice for y'. I get failed just cos I'm more well read than the friggin' examiner!

FRANK   Devouring pulp fiction is not being well read.

RITA   I thought reading was supposed to be good for one. (*She gets out her cigarettes*)

FRANK   It is, but you've got to be selective. In your favour you do mention *Sons and Lovers* somewhere in here. When did you read that?

RITA This week. I read that an' the Harold Robbins an' this dead fantastic book, what was it called? Erm—ogh what was it? It sounded like somethin' dead perverted, it was by that English feller ...

FRANK Which English feller?

RITA You know, the one who was like Noël Coward—erm. Oh, I know—Somerset Maughan.

FRANK A perverted book by Somerset Maugham?

RITA No, it wasn't perverted it was great—the title sounds perverted ...

He starts to laugh

Don't laugh.

FRANK Do you mean *Of Human Bondage*?

RITA Yeh—that's it. Well it does sound perverted doesn't it?

FRANK Well! (*After a pause*) You read three novels this week?

RITA (*taking a cigarette from the pack*) Yeh. It was dead quiet in the shop.

FRANK And if I asked you to make a comparison between those books, what would you say?

RITA Well, they were all good in their own way.

FRANK But surely you can see the difference between the Harold Robbins and the other two.

RITA Apart from that one bein' American like?

FRANK Yes.

RITA Yeh. I mean the other two were sort of posher. But they're all books, aren't they?

FRANK Yes. Yes. But you seem to be under the impression that all books are literature.

RITA Aren't they?

FRANK No.

RITA Well—well how d' y' tell?

FRANK I—erm—erm—one's always known really.

RITA But how d' y' work it out if y' don't know? See that's what I've got to learn, isn't it? I'm dead ignorant y' know.

25

FRANK   No. You're not ignorant. It's merely a question of becoming discerning in your choice of reading material.

RITA   I've got no taste. Is that what you're saying?

FRANK   No.

RITA   It is. Don't worry. I won't get upset. I'm here to learn. My mind's full of junk, isn't it? It needs a good clearin' out. Right, that's it, I'll never read a Robbins novel again.

FRANK   Read it, by all means read it. But don't mention it in an exam.

RITA   Aha. You mean, it's all right to go out an' have a bit of slap an' tickle with the lads as long as you don't go home an' tell your mum?

FRANK   Erm—well yes, that's probably what I do mean.

Black-out

RITA *exits*

Scene four

The lights come up on FRANK *who is standing by the window*

RITA *enters and shuts the door behind her, standing just inside the room*

FRANK *goes to his briefcase on the window-desk and starts looking for Rita's 'Peer Gynt' essay*

RITA   I can't do it. Honest, I just can't understand what he's on about. (*She goes to her chair at the desk, dumps her bag and then goes and hangs up her coat*) He's got me licked, I don't know what he's on about, 'Only connect, only connect', it's just bleedin' borin'. It's no good, I just can't understand.

FRANK   You will. You will.

RITA   It's all right for you sayin' that. You know what it's about. (*She goes to her chair by the desk*) But I just can't figure it.

FRANK   Do you think we could forget about Forster for a moment?

RITA   With pleasure.

FRANK *takes the 'Peer Gynt' essay and stands over her for a moment. Then he perches on the corner of the desk* UL

FRANK   I want to talk about this that you sent me. (*He holds up a sheet of A4 paper*)

RITA   That? Oh.

FRANK   Yes. In response to the question, 'Suggest how you would resolve the staging difficulties inherent in a production of Ibsen's Peer Gynt', you have written, quote, 'Do it on the radio', unquote.

RITA   Precisely.

FRANK   Well?

RITA   Well what?

FRANK   Well I know it's probably quite naïve of me but I did think you might let me have a considered essay.

RITA *sits down by the desk and unpacks the student's pad, pencil case, ruler, copy of 'Peer Gynt' and eight reference books from her bag*

RITA   That's all I could do in the time. We were dead busy in the shop this week.

FRANK   You write your essays at work?

RITA   Yeh.

FRANK   Why?

RITA   Denny get's dead narked if I work at home. He doesn't like me doin' this. I can't be bothered arguin' with him.

FRANK   But you can't go on producing work as thin as this.

RITA   Is it wrong?

FRANK   No, it's not wrong, it's just ...

RITA   See, I know it's short. But I thought it was the right answer.

FRANK   It's the basis for an argument, Rita, but one line is hardly an essay.

RITA   I know, but I didn't have much time this week, so I sort of, y' know, encapsulated all me ideas in one line.

FRANK   But it's not enough.

RITA   Why not?

FRANK   It just isn't.

RITA   But that's bleedin' stupid, cos you say—you say, don't y'—that one line of exquisite poetry says more than a thousand pages of second-rate prose?

FRANK   But you're not writing poetry. What I'm trying to make you see is that whoever was marking this would want more than, 'Do it on the radio'. (*He gets up and moves around to the other side of Rita's chair*) There is a way of answering examination questions that is expected. It's a sort of accepted ritual, it's a game, with rules. And you must observe those rules. (*He leans with one hand on the back of Rita's chair*) When I was at university there was a student taking his final theology exam. He walked into the examination hall, took out his pen and wrote 'God knows all the answers', then he handed in his paper and left.

RITA   (*impressed*) Did he?

FRANK   When his paper was returned to him, his professor had written on it, 'And God gives out the marks'.

RITA   Did he fail?

FRANK   (*breaking away slightly*) Of course he failed. You see, a clever answer is not necessarily the correct answer.

RITA   (*getting out her cigarettes*) I wasn't tryin' to be clever; I didn't have much time an' I ...

FRANK   All right, but look, you've got some time now. (*He leans on her chair, bending over her*) Just give it a quarter of an hour or so adding some considered argument to this: 'In attempting to resolve the staging difficulties in *Peer Gynt* I would present it on the radio because ...' and outline your reasons supporting them, as much as possible, with quotes from accepted authorities. All right?

RITA   Yeh. All right (*She picks up the essay, pen, copy of 'Peer Gynt', eight reference books, sticks the cigarette in her mouth, and starts to move towards the window desk*)

FRANK   Now, are you sure you understand?

RITA *stops and speaks over her shoulder with the cigarette still in her mouth*

RITA Yeh. What d' y' think I am, thick? (*She takes her usual chair and puts it in front of the window desk. She sits down and puts her belongings on the desk, moving Frank's briefcase out of the way*)

FRANK *moves the swivel chair to the U end of his desk and settles down to marking essays*

RITA *leans back in the chair and tries to blow smoke-rings*

Y' know Peer Gynt? He was searchin' for the meaning of life wasn't he?

FRANK Erm—put at its briefest, yes.

RITA Yeh. (*She pauses*) I was doin' this woman's hair on Wednesday ...

FRANK Tch ...

RITA (*facing* FRANK) I'm gonna do this, don't worry. I'll do it. But I just wanna tell y'; I was doin' her hair an' I was dead bored with what the others in the shop were talkin' about. So I just said to this woman, I said, 'Do you know about *Peer Gynt*?' She thought it was a new perm lotion. So I told her all about it, y' know the play. An' y' know somethin', she was dead interested, she was y' know.

FRANK Was she?

RITA Yeh. She said, 'I wish I could go off searchin' for the meanin' of life.' There's loads of them round by us who feel like that. Cos by us there is no meanin' to life. (*She thinks*) Frank, y' know culture, y' know the word culture? Well it doesn't just mean goin' to the opera an' that, does it?

FRANK No.

RITA It means a way of livin', doesn't it? Well we've got no culture.

FRANK Of course you have.

RITA What? Do you mean like that working-class culture thing?

FRANK Mm.

RITA Yeh. I've read about that. I've never seen it though.

FRANK   Well, look around you.

RITA   I do. But I don't see any, y' know, culture. I just see everyone pissed, or on the Valium, tryin' to get from one day to the next. Y' daren't say that round our way like, cos they're proud. They'll tell y' they've got culture as they sit there drinkin' their keg beer out of plastic glasses.

FRANK   Yes, but there's nothing wrong with that, if they're content with it.

During the following FRANK'S *attention is caught gradually and he stops marking and starts listening*

RITA   But they're not. Cos there's no meanin'. They tell y' stories about the past, y' know, the war, or when they were fightin' for food an' clothin' an' houses. Their eyes light up as they tell y', because there was some meanin' to it. But the thing is that now, I mean now that most of them have got some sort of house an' there's food an' money around, they know they're better off but, honest, they know they've got nothin' as well. There's like this sort of disease, but no one mentions it; everyone behaves as though it's normal, y' know inevitable that there's vandalism an' violence an' houses burnt out an' wrecked by the people they were built for. There's somethin' wrong. An' like the worst thing is that y' know the people who are supposed to like represent the people on our estate, y' know the *Daily Mirror* an' the *Sun*, an' ITV an' the Unions, what are they tellin' people to do? They just tell them to go out an' get more money, don't they? But they don't want more money; it's like me, isn't it? Y' know, buyin' new dresses all the time, isn't it? The Unions tell them to go out an' get more money an' ITV an' the papers tell them what to spend it on so the disease is always covered up.

FRANK *swivels round in his chair to face* RITA

FRANK   (*after a pause*) Why didn't you take a course in politics?

RITA   Politics? Go way, I hate politics. I'm just tellin' y' about round our way. I wanna be on this course findin' out. You know what I learn from you, about art an' literature, it feeds me, inside. I can get through the rest of the week if I know I've got comin' here to look forward to. Denny tried to stop me comin' tonight. He tried to get me to go out to the pub with him an' his mates. He hates me comin' here. It's like drug addicts, isn't it? They hate it when one of them tries to break away. It makes me stronger comin' here. That's what Denny's frightened of.

FRANK 'Only connect.'

RITA Oh, not friggin' Forster again.

FRANK 'Only connect.' You see what you've been doing?

RITA Just tellin' y' about home.

FRANK Yes, and connecting, your dresses/ITV and the *Daily Mirror*. Addicts/you and your husband.

RITA Ogh!

FRANK You see?

RITA An'—an' in that book—no one does connect.

FRANK Irony.

RITA Is that it? Is that all it means?

FRANK Yes.

RITA Why didn't y' just tell me, right from the start?

FRANK I could have told you; but you'll have a much better understanding of something if you discover it in your own terms.

RITA (*sincerely*) Aren't you clever?

FRANK Brilliant. Now. *Peer Gynt*.

RITA All right, all right, hold on. (*She opens a couple of books and starts writing*)

FRANK *continues his marking and does not notice as* RITA *finishes writing. She picks up her chair, essay, pen and books, and moves across in front of his desk. She replaces the chair by the desk and stands watching him*

FRANK (*looking up*) What?

RITA I've done it.

FRANK You've done it?

She hands him the essay

(*Reading aloud*) 'In attempting to resolve the

31

staging difficulties in a production of Ibsen's *Peer Gynt* I would present it on the radio because as Ibsen himself says, he wrote the play as a play for voices, never intending it to go on in a theatre. If they had the radio in his day that's where he would have done it.'

He looks up as she beams him a satisfied smile

Black-out

Scene five

As the lights come up FRANK *is sitting in the swivel chair and* RITA *stands by the filing cabinet*

FRANK What's wrong? (*After a pause*) You know this is getting to be a bit wearisome. When you come to this room you'll do anything except start work immediately. Couldn't you just come in prepared to start work? Where's your essay?

RITA (*staring out of the window*) I haven't got it.

FRANK You haven't done it?

RITA I said I haven't got it.

FRANK You've lost it?

RITA It's burnt.

FRANK Burnt?

RITA So are all the Chekhov books you lent me. Denny found out I was on the pill again; it was my fault, I left me prescription out. He burnt all me books.

FRANK Oh Christ!

RITA I'm sorry. I'll buy y' some more.

FRANK I wasn't referring to the books. Sod the books.

RITA Why can't he just let me get on with me learnin'? You'd think I was havin' a bloody affair the way he behaves.

FRANK And aren't you?

RITA *wanders* DR. *She fiddles with the library steps, smoothing the top step*

RITA (*looking at him*) No. What time have I got for an affair?

I'm busy enough findin' meself, let alone findin' someone else. I don't want anyone else. I've begun to find me—an' it's great y' know, it is Frank. It might sound selfish but all I want for the time bein' is what I'm findin' inside me. I certainly don't wanna be rushin' off with some feller, cos the first thing I'll have to do is forget about meself for the sake of him.

FRANK Perhaps, perhaps your husband thinks you're having an affair with me.

RITA Oh go way. You're me teacher. I've told him.

FRANK You've told him about me? What?

RITA (sitting down) I've—tch—I've tried to explain to him how you give me room to breathe. Y' just, like feed me without expectin' anythin' in return.

FRANK What did he say?

RITA He didn't. I was out for a while. When I come back he'd burnt me books an' papers, most of them. I said to him, y' soft get, even if I was havin' an affair there's no point burnin' me books. I'm not havin' it off with Anton Chekhov. He said, 'I wouldn't put it past you to shack up with a foreigner'.

FRANK (after a pause) What are you going to do?

RITA I'll order some new copies for y' an' do the essay again.

FRANK I mean about your husband.

RITA (standing up) I've told him, I said, 'There's no point cryin' over spilt milk, most of the books are gone, but if you touch my *Peer Gynt* I'll kill y'.'

FRANK Tch. Be serious.

RITA I was!

FRANK Do you love him?

RITA (after a pause) I see him lookin' at me sometimes, an' I know what he's thinkin, I do y' know, he's wonderin' where the girl he married has gone to. He even brings me presents sometimes, hopin' that the presents 'll make her come back. But she can't, because she's gone, an' I've taken her place.

FRANK Do you want to abandon this course?

33

RITA No. No!

FRANK When art and literature begin to take the place of life itself, perhaps it's time to ...

RITA (*emphatically*) But it's not takin' the place of life, it's providin' me with life itself. He wants to take life away from me; he wants me to stop rockin' the coffin, that's all. Comin' here, doin' this, it's given me more life then I've had in years, an' he should be able to see that. Well, if he doesn't want me when I'm alive I'm certainly not just gonna lie down an' die for him. I told him I'd only have a baby when I had choice. But he doesn't understand. He thinks we've got choice because we can go into a pub that sells eight different kinds of lager. He thinks we've got choice already: choice between Everton an' Liverpool, choosin' which washin' powder, choosin' between one lousy school an' the next, between lousy jobs or the dole, choosin' between Stork an' butter.

FRANK Yes. Well, perhaps your husband ...

RITA No. I don't wanna talk about him. (*She comes to the front of the desk*) Why was Chekhov a comic genius?

FRANK Rita. Don't you think that for tonight we could give the class a miss?

RITA No. I wanna know. I've got to do this. He can burn me books an' me papers but if it's all in me head he can't touch it. It's like that with you, isn't it? You've got it all inside.

FRANK Let's leave it for tonight. Let's go to the pub and drink pots of Guinness and talk.

RITA I've got to do this, Frank. I've got to. I want to talk about Chekhov.

FRANK We really should talk about you and Denny, my dear.

RITA I don't want to.

FRANK (*after a pause*) All right. Chekhov.

RITA *goes to the u end of the desk and stands between the chair and the desk*

FRANK 'C' for Chekhov.

He gets up and moves towards the bookcase, taking Rita's chair with him. He stands on the chair and begins rummaging on the top shelf, dropping some of the books on the floor. RITA *turns to sit down and notices her chair has gone. She sees* FRANK *and watches him as he finds a bottle of whisky hidden behind some books. He gets down and takes the whisky to the small table*

We'll talk about Chekhov and pretend this is the pub.

RITA Why d' y' keep it stashed behind there?

FRANK (*pouring the drinks*) A little arrangement I have with my immediate employers. It's called discretion. They didn't tell me to stop drinking, they told me to stop displaying the signs.

RITA (*climbing on to the chair to replace the books*) Do you actually like drinking?

FRANK Oh yes. I love it. Absolutely no guilt at all about it.

RITA Know when you were a poet, Frank, did y' drink then?

FRANK Some. Not as much as now. (*He takes a drink*) You see, the great thing about the booze is that it makes one believe that under all the talk one is actually saying something.

RITA Why did you stop bein' a poet?

FRANK (*wagging his finger at her*) That is a pub question.

RITA Well. I thought we were pretendin' this was the pub. (*She gets down from the chair*)

FRANK In which we would discuss Chekhov.

RITA Well he's second on the bill. You're on first. Go on, why did y' stop?

FRANK I didn't stop, so much as realize I never was. I'd simply got it wrong, Rita. (*After a pause*) Instead of creating poetry I spent—oh—years and years trying to create literature. You see?

RITA (*replacing her chair* U *of the desk*) Well I thought that's what poets did.

FRANK What? (*He gives* RITA *her drink*)

RITA Y' know, make literature. (*She perches on the small table*)

FRANK (*shaking his head*) Poets shouldn't believe in literature.

RITA (*puzzled*) I don't understand that.

FRANK You will. You will.

RITA Sometimes I wonder if I'll ever understand any of it. It's like startin' all over again, y' know with a different language. Know I read that Chekhov play an' I thought it was dead sad, it was tragic; people committin' suicide an' that Constantin kid's tryin' to produce his masterpiece an' they're all laughin' at him? It's tragic. Then I read the blurb on it an' everyone's goin' on about Chekhov bein' a comic genius.

FRANK Well, it's not comedy like—erm—well it's not stand-up comedy. Have you ever seen Chekhov in the theatre?

RITA No. Does he go?

FRANK Have you ever been to the theatre?

RITA No.

FRANK You should go.

RITA (*standing up*) Hey! Why don't we go tonight?

FRANK Me? Go to the theatre? God no, I hate the theatre.

RITA Why the hell are y' sendin' me?

FRANK Because you want to know.

RITA (*packing her things into her bag*) Well, you come with me.

FRANK And how would I explain that to Julia?

RITA Just tell her y' comin' to the theatre with me.

FRANK 'Julia, I shall not be in for dinner as I am going to the theatre with ravishing Rita.'

RITA Oh sod off.

FRANK I'm being quite serious.

RITA Would she really be jealous?

FRANK If she knew I was at the theatre with an irresistible thing like you? Rita, it would be deaf and dumb breakfasts for a week.

RITA Why?

FRANK Why not?

RITA I dunno—I just thought ...

FRANK (*pouring himself another drink*) Rita, ludicrous as it may seem to you, even a woman who possesses an M.A. is not above common jealousy.

RITA Well, what's she got to be jealous of me for? I'm not gonna try an' rape y' in the middle of *The Seagull*.

FRANK What an awful pity. You could have made theatre exciting for me again.

RITA Come on, Frank. Come with me. Y' never tell the truth you, do y'?

FRANK What d' y' mean?

RITA Y' don't; y' like evade it with jokes an' that, don't y'? Come on, come to the theatre with me. We'll have a laugh ...

FRANK Will we?

RITA Yeh. C'mon we'll ring Julia. (*She goes to the telephone and picks up the receiver*)

FRANK What!

RITA C'mon, what's your number?

FRANK (*taking the receiver from her and replacing it*) We will not ring Julia. Anyway Julia's out tonight.

RITA So what will you do, spend the night in the pub?

FRANK Yes.

RITA Come with me, Frank, y'll have a better time than y' will in the pub.

FRANK Will I?

RITA Course y' will. (*She goes and gets both coats from the hook by the door, comes back and throws her coat over the back of the chair*)

FRANK (*putting down his mug on the bookcase*) What is it you want to see?

RITA *helps* FRANK *into his coat*

RITA *The Importance of Bein' Thingy* ...

FRANK But *The Importance* isn't playing at the moment ...

RITA It is—I passed the church hall on the bus an' there was a poster ...

FRANK *breaks loose, turns to her and throws off his coat*

FRANK (*aghast*) An amateur production?

37

RITA What?

FRANK Are you suggesting I miss a night at the pub to watch *The Importance* played by amateurs in a church hall?

RITA *picks his coat up and puts it round his shoulders*

RITA Yeh. It doesn't matter who's doin' it, does it? It's the same play, isn't it?

FRANK Possibly, Rita ... (*He switches off the desk lamp*)

RITA (*putting on her coat and picking up her bag*) Well come on—hurry up—I'm dead excited. I've never seen a live play before.

FRANK *goes round switching off the electric fire and desk lamp and then picks up his briefcase*

FRANK And there's no guarantee you'll see a 'live' play tonight.

RITA Why? Just cos they're amateurs? Y've gorra give them a chance. They have to learn somewhere. An' they might be good.

FRANK (*doubtfully*) Yes ...

RITA Oh y' an awful snob, aren't y'?

FRANK (*smiling acknowledgement*) All right—come on.

They go towards the door

RITA Have you seen it before?

FRANK Of course.

RITA Well, don't go tellin' me what happens will y'? Don't go spoilin' it for me.

FRANK *switches off the light switch. Black-out*

FRANK *and* RITA *exit*

Scene six

The lights come up

FRANK *enters carrying a briefcase and a pile of essays. He goes to the filing cabinet, takes his lecture notes from the briefcase and puts them in a drawer. He takes the sandwiches and apple from his briefcase and puts them on his desk and then goes to the window desk and dumps the essays and briefcase. He switches on the radio and then sits in the swivel chair. He opens the packet of sandwiches, takes a bite and then picks up a book and starts reading*

RITA *bursts through the door out of breath*

FRANK   What are you doing here? (*He looks at his watch*) It's Thursday, you ...

RITA   (*moving over to the desk; quickly*) I know I shouldn't be here, it's me dinner hour, but listen, I've gorra tell someone, have y' got a few minutes, can y' spare ...?

FRANK   (*alarmed*) My God, what is it?

RITA   I had to come an' tell y', Frank, last night, I went to the theatre! A proper one, a professional theatre.

Frank gets up and switches off the radio and then returns to the swivel chair

FRANK   (*sighing*) For God's sake, you had me worried, I thought it was something serious.

RITA   No, listen, it was. I went out an' got me ticket, it was Shakespeare, I thought it was gonna be dead borin' ...

FRANK   Then why did you go in the first place?

RITA   I wanted to find out. But listen, it wasn't borin', it was bleedin' great, honest, ogh, it done me in, it was fantastic. I'm gonna do an essay on it.

FRANK   (*smiling*) Come on, which one was it?

RITA *moves* URC

RITA   '... Out, out, brief candle!
        Life's but a walking shadow, a poor player
        That struts and frets his hour upon the stage
        And then is heard no more. It is a tale
        Told by an idiot, full of sound and fury
        Signifying nothing.'

FRANK   (*deliberately*) Ah, *Romeo and Juliet*.

RITA   (*moving towards* FRANK) Tch. Frank! Be serious. I learnt that today from the book. (*She produces a copy of*

'Macbeth') Look, I went out an' bought the book. Isn't it great? What I couldn't get over is how excitin' it was.

FRANK *puts his feet up on the desk*

RITA Wasn't his wife a cow, eh? An' that fantastic bit where he meets Macduff an' he thinks he's all invincible. I was on the edge of me seat at that bit. I wanted to shout out an' tell Macbeth, warn him.

FRANK You didn't, did you?

RITA Nah. Y' can't do that in a theatre, can y'? It was dead good. It was like a thriller.

FRANK Yes. You'll have to go and see more.

RITA I'm goin' to. Macbeth's a tragedy, isn't it?

FRANK *nods*

RITA Right.

RITA *smiles at* FRANK *and he smiles back at her*

Well I just—I just had to tell someone who'd understand.

FRANK I'm honoured that you chose me.

RITA (*moving towards the door*) Well, I better get back. I've left a customer with a perm lotion. If I don't get a move on there'll be another tragedy.

FRANK No. There won't be a tragedy.

RITA There will, y' know. I know this woman; she's dead fussy. If her perm doesn't come out right there'll be blood an' guts everywhere.

FRANK Which might be quite tragic—

He throws her the apple from his desk which she catches

—but it won't be a tragedy.

RITA What?

FRANK Well—erm—look; the tragedy of the drama has nothing to do with the sort of tragic event you're talking about. Macbeth is flawed by his ambition—yes?

RITA (*going and sitting in the chair by the desk*) Yeh. Go on. (*She starts to eat the apple*)

FRANK Erm—it's that flaw which forces him to take the inevitable steps towards his own doom. You see?

RITA *offers him the can of soft drink. He takes it and looks at it*

FRANK   (*putting the can down on the desk*) No thanks. Whereas, Rita, a woman's hair being reduced to an inch of stubble, or—or the sort of thing you read in the paper that's reported as being tragic, 'Man Killed By Falling Tree', is not a tragedy.

RITA   It is for the poor sod under the tree.

FRANK   Yes, it's tragic, absolutely tragic. But it's not a tragedy in the way that *Macbeth* is a tragedy. Tragedy in dramatic terms is inevitable, pre-ordained. Look, now, even without ever having heard the story of *Macbeth* you wanted to shout out, to warn him and prevent him going on, didn't you? But you wouldn't have been able to stop him would you?

RITA   No.

FRANK   Why?

RITA   They would have thrown me out the theatre.

FRANK   But what I mean is that your warning would have been ignored. He's warned in the play. But he can't go back. He still treads the path to doom. But the poor old fellow under the tree hasn't arrived there by following any inevitable steps has he?

RITA   No.

FRANK   There's no particular flaw in his character that has dictated his end. If he'd been warned of the consequences of standing beneath that particular tree he wouldn't have done it, would he? Understand.

RITA   So—so Macbeth brings it on himself?

FRANK   Yes. You see he goes blindly on and on and with every step he's spinning one more piece of thread which will eventually make up the network of his own tragedy. Do you see?

RITA   I think so. I'm not used to thinkin' like this.

FRANK   It's quite easy, Rita.

RITA   It is for you. I just thought it was a dead excitin' story. But the way you tell it you make me see all sorts of things in it. (*After a pause*) It's fun, tragedy, isn't it? (*She goes over to the window*) All them out there, they know all about that sort of thing don't they?

41

FRANK   Look, how about a proper lunch?

RITA   Lunch? (*She leaps up, grabs the copy of 'Macbeth', the can of drink and the apple and goes to the door*) Christ—me customer. She only wanted a demi-wave—she'll come out looking like a friggin' muppet (*She comes back to the table*) Ey' Frank, listen—I was thinkin of goin' to the art gallery tomorrow. It's me half-day off. D' y' wanna come with me?

FRANK   (*smiling*) All right.

RITA *goes to the door*

FRANK   (*looking at her*) And—look, what are you doing on Saturday?

RITA   I work.

FRANK   Well, when you finish work.

RITA   Dunno.

FRANK   I want you to come over to the house.

RITA   Why?

FRANK   Julia's organized a few people to come round for dinner.

RITA   An' y' want me to come? Why?

FRANK   Why do you think?

RITA   I dunno.

FRANK   Because you might enjoy it.

RITA   Oh.

FRANK   Will you come?

RITA   If y' want.

FRANK   What do you want?

RITA   All right. I'll come.

FRANK   Will you bring Denny?

RITA   I don't know if he'll come.

FRANK   Well ask him.

RITA   (*puzzled*) All right.

FRANK   What's wrong?

RITA   What shall I wear?

Black-out

RITA *goes out*

Scene seven

The lights come up on FRANK *who is sitting in the armchair listening to the radio*

RITA *enters, goes straight to the desk and slings her bag on the back of her chair*

She sits in the chair and unpacks the note-pad and pencil-case from her bag. She opens the pad and takes out the pencil-sharpener and pencils and arranges them as before. FRANK *gets up, switches off the radio, goes to the swivel chair and sits*

FRANK Now I don't mind; two empty seats at the dinner table means more of the vino for me. But Julia—Julia is the stage-manager type. If we're having eight people to dinner she expects to see eight. She likes order—probably why she took me on—it gives her a lot of practice—

RITA *starts sharpening her pencils*

FRANK —and having to cope with six instead of eight was extremely hard on Julia. I'm not saying that I needed any sort of apology; you don't turn up that's up to you, but ...

RITA I did apologize.

FRANK 'Sorry couldn't come', scribbled on the back of your essay and thrust through the letter box? Rita, that's hardly an apology.

RITA What does the word 'sorry' mean if it's not an apology? When I told Denny we were goin' to yours he went mad. We had a big fight about it.

FRANK I'm sorry. I didn't realize. But look, couldn't you have explained? Couldn't you have said that was the reason?

RITA No. Cos that wasn't the reason. I told Denny if he wasn't gonna go I'd go on me own. An' I tried to. All day Saturday, all day in the shop I was thinkin' what to wear. I got back, an' I tried on five different dresses. They all looked bleedin' awful. An' all the time I'm trying to think of things

43

I can say, what I can talk about. An' I can't remember anythin'. It's all jumbled up in me head. I can't remember if it's Wilde who's witty an' Shaw who was Shavian or who the hell wrote *Howards End*.

FRANK Ogh God!

RITA Then I got the wrong bus to your house. It took me ages to find it. Then I walked up your drive, an' I saw y' all through the window, y' were sippin' drinks an' talkin' an' laughin'. An' I couldn't come in.

FRANK Of course you could.

RITA I couldn't. I'd bought the wrong sort of wine. When I was in the off licence I knew I was buyin' the wrong stuff. But I didn't know which was the right wine.

FRANK Rita for Christ's sake; I wanted *you* to come along. You weren't expected to dress up or buy wine.

RITA (*holding all the pencils and pens in her hands and playing with them*) If you go out to dinner don't you dress up? Don't you take wine?

FRANK Yes, but ...

RITA Well?

FRANK Well what?

RITA Well you wouldn't take sweet sparkling wine, would y'?

FRANK Does it matter what I do? It wouldn't have mattered if you'd walked in with a bottle of Spanish plonk.

RITA It was Spanish.

FRANK Why couldn't you relax? (*He gets up and goes behind Rita's chair, then leans on the back of it*) It wasn't a fancy dress party. You could have come as yourself. Don't you realize how people would have seen you if you'd just—just breezed in? Mm? They would have seen someone who's funny, delightful, charming ...

RITA (*angrily*) But I don't wanna be charming and delightful: funny. What's funny? I don't wanna be funny. I wanna talk seriously with the rest of you, I don't wanna spend the night takin' the piss, comin' on with the funnies because that's the only way I can get into the conversation. I didn't want to come to your house just to play the court jester.

FRANK You weren't being asked to play that role. I just—just wanted you to be yourself.

RITA But I don't want to be myself. Me? What's me? Some stupid woman who gives us all a laugh because she thinks she can learn, because she thinks that one day she'll be like the rest of them, talking seriously, confidently, with knowledge, livin' a civilized life. Well, she can't be like that really but bring her in because she's good for a laugh!

FRANK If you believe that that's why you were invited, to be laughed at, then you can get out, now. (*He goes to his desk and grabs the pile of essays, taking them to the window desk. He stands with his back to* RITA *and starts pushing the essays into his briefcase*) You were invited because I wished to have your company and if you can't believe that then I suggest you stop visiting me and start visiting an analyst who can cope with paranoia.

RITA I'm all right with you, here in this room; but when I saw those people you were with I couldn't come in. I would have seized up. Because I'm a freak. I can't talk to the people I live with any more. An' I can't talk to the likes of them on Saturday, or them out there, because I can't learn the language. I'm a half-caste. I went back to the pub where Denny was, an' me mother, an' our Sandra, an' her mates. I'd decided I wasn't comin' here again.

FRANK *turns to face her*

RITA I went into the pub an' they were singin', all of them singin' some song they'd learnt from the juke-box. An' I stood in that pub an' thought, just what the frig am I trying to do? Why don't I just pack it in an' stay with them, an' join in the singin'?

FRANK And why don't you?

RITA (*angrily*) You think I can, don't you? Just because you pass a pub doorway an' hear the singin' you think we're all O. K., that we're all survivin', with the spirit intact. Well I did join in with the singin', I didn't ask any questions, I just went along with it.

45

But when I looked round me mother had stopped singin', an' she was cryin', but no one could get it out of her why she was cryin'. Everyone just said she was pissed an' we should get her home. So we did, an' on the way I asked her why. I said, 'Why are y' cryin', Mother?' She said, 'Because—because we could sing better songs than those.' Ten minutes later, Denny had her laughing and singing again, pretending she hadn't said it. But she had. And that's why I came back. And that's why I'm staying.

Black-out

RITA *goes out*

Scene eight

The lights come up on FRANK *seated in the swivel chair at the desk reading Rita's 'Macbeth' essay*

RITA *enters slowly, carrying a suitcase*

FRANK   (*without looking up*) One second.

She puts down the suitcase RC *and wanders slowly* R *with her back to* FRANK

(*He closes the essay he has been reading, sighs and removes his glasses*) Your essay. (*He sees the suitcase*) What's that?

RITA   It's me case.

FRANK   Where are you going?

RITA   Me mother's.

FRANK   What's wrong? (*After a pause*) Rita!

RITA   I got home from work, he'd packed me case. He said either I stop comin' here an' come off the pill or I could get out altogether.

FRANK   Tch.

RITA   It was an ultimatum. I explained to him. I didn't get narked or anythin'. I just explained to him how I had to do

46

this. He said it's warped me. He said I'd betrayed him. I suppose I have.

FRANK Why have you?

RITA I have. I know he's right. But I couldn't betray meself. (*After a pause*) He says there's a time for education. An' it's not when y' twenty-six an' married.

FRANK *gets up and goes towards* RITA *who still faces away from him*

FRANK (*after a pause*) Where are you going to stay?

RITA I phoned me mother; she said I could go there for a week. Then I'll get a flat. (*She starts to cry*) I'm sorry, it's just ...

FRANK *takes hold of her and tries to guide her to the chair* DR

FRANK Look, come on, sit down.

RITA (*breaking away from him*) It's all right—I'll be O. K. Just give me a minute. (*She dries her eyes*) What was me *Macbeth* essay like?

FRANK Oh sod *Macbeth*.

RITA Why?

FRANK Rita!

RITA No, come on, come on, I want y' to tell me what y' thought about it.

FRANK In the circumstances ...

RITA (*going and hanging her bag on the back of the swivel chair*) It doesn't matter, it doesn't; in the circumstances I need to go on, to talk about it an' do it. What was it like? I told y' it was no good. Is it really useless?

FRANK *sits in the chair* DR

FRANK (*sighing*) I—I really don't know what to say.

RITA Well try an' think of somethin'. Go on, I don't mind if y' tell me it was rubbish. I don't want pity, Frank. Was it rubbish?

FRANK No, no. It's not rubbish. It's a totally honest, passionate account of your reaction to a play. It's an unashamedly emotional statement about a certain experience.

RITA Sentimental?

FRANK No. It's too honest for that. It's almost—erm—

47

moving. But in terms of what you're asking me to teach you of passing exams ... Oh, God, you see, I don't ...

RITA Say it, go on, say it!

FRANK In those terms it's worthless. It shouldn't be, but it is; in it's own terms it's—it's wonderful.

RITA (*confronting him across the desk*) It's worthless! You said. An' if it's worthless you've got to tell me because I wanna write essays like those on there. (*She points to the essays on the desk*) I wanna know, an' pass exams like they do.

FRANK But if you're going to write this sort of stuff you're going to have to change.

RITA All right. Tell me how to do it.

FRANK (*getting up*) But I don't know if I want to tell you, Rita, I don't know that I want to teach you. (*He moves towards the desk*) What you already have is valuable.

RITA Valuable? What's valuable? The only thing I value is here, comin' here once a week.

FRANK But, don't you see, if you're going to write this sort of thing—(*he indicates the pile of essays*)— to pass examinations, you're going to have to suppress, perhaps even abandon your uniqueness. I'm going to have to change you.

RITA But don't you realize, I want to change! Listen, is this your way of tellin' me that I can't do it? That I'm no good?

FRANK It's not that at ...

RITA If that's what you're trying' to tell me I'll go now ...

FRANK *turns away from her*

FRANK (*moving away from the desk*) No no no. Of course you're good enough.

RITA See I know it's difficult for y' with someone like me. But you've just gorra keep tellin' me an' then I'll start to take it in; y' see, with me you've got to be dead firm. You won't hurt me feelings y' know. If I do somethin' that's crap, I don't want pity, you just tell me, that's crap. (*She picks up the essay*) Here, it's crap. (*She rips it up*) Right. So we dump that in the bin, (*She does so*) an' we start again.

Act Two

Scene one

When the curtain rises FRANK *is sitting at his desk typing poetry. He pauses, stubs out a cigarette, takes a sip from the mug at his side, looks at his watch and then continues typing*

RITA *bursts through the door. She is dressed in new, second-hand clothes*

RITA Frank! (*She twirls on the spot to show off her new clothes*)

FRANK (*smiling*) And what is this vision, returning from the city? (*He gets up and moves towards* RITA) Welcome back.

RITA Frank, it was fantastic.

She takes off her shawl and gives it to FRANK *who hangs it on the hook by the door.* RITA *goes to the desk*

 (*Putting down her bag on the desk*) Honest, it was—ogh!

FRANK What are you talking about, London or summer school?

RITA Both. A crowd of us stuck together all week. We had a great time: dead late every night, we stayed up talkin', we went all round London, got drunk, went to the theatres, bought all sorts of second-hand gear in the markets ... Ogh, it was ...

FRANK So you won't have had time to do any actual work there?

RITA Work? We never stopped. Lashin' us with it they were; another essay, lash, do it again, lash.

FRANK *moves towards the desk*

RITA Another lecture, smack. It was dead good though. (*She goes and perches on the bookcase* UR)

FRANK *sits in the swivel chair, facing her*

RITA Y' know at first I was dead scared. I didn't know anyone. I was gonna come home. But the first afternoon I was standin' in this library, y' know lookin' at the books,

49

pretendin' I was dead clever. Anyway, this tutor come up to me, he looked at the book in me hand an' he said, 'Ah, are you fond of Ferlinghetti?' It was right on the tip of me tongue to say, 'Only when it's served with Parmesan cheese', but, Frank, I didn't. I held it back an' I heard meself sayin', 'Actually, I'm not too familiar with the American poets'. Frank, you woulda been dead proud of me. He started talkin' to me about the American poets—we sat around for ages—an' he wasn't even one of my official tutors, y' know. We had to go to this big hall for a lecture, there must have been two thousand of us in there. After he'd finished his lecture this professor asked if anyone had a question, an', Frank, I stood up! (*She stands*) Honest to God, I stood up, an' everyone's lookin' at me. I don't know what possessed me, I was gonna sit down again, but two thousand people had seen me stand up, so I did it, I asked him the question.

There is a pause and FRANK *waits*

FRANK Well?

RITA Well what?

FRANK What was the question?

RITA Oh, I dunno, I forget now, cos after that I was askin' questions all week, y' couldn't keep me down. I think that first question was about Chekhov; cos y' know I'm dead familiar with Chekhov now.

He smiles. RITA *moves to the chair by the desk and sits.* FRANK *swivels round to face her*

Hey, what was France like? Go on, tell us all about it.

FRANK There isn't a lot to tell.

RITA Ah go on, tell me about it; I've never been abroad. Tell me what it was like.

FRANK Well—it was rather hot ... (*He offers her a Gauloise*)

RITA No, ta, I've packed it in. Did y' drink?

FRANK Ah—a little. (*He puts the cigarettes on the table*)

RITA Tch. Did y' write?

FRANK A little.

RITA Will y' show it to me?

FRANK   Perhaps ... One day, perhaps.

RITA   So y' wrote a bit an' y' drank a bit? Is that all?

FRANK   (*in a matter of fact tone*) Julia left me.

RITA   What?

FRANK   Yes. But not because of the obvious, oh no—it had nothing whatsoever to do with the ratatouille. It was actually caused by something called *oeufs en cocotte*.

RITA   What?

FRANK   Eggs, my dear, eggs. Nature in her wisdom cursed me with a dislike for the egg be it cocotte, Florentine, Benedict or plain hard-boiled. Julia insisted that nature was wrong. I defended nature and Julia left.

RITA   Because of eggs?

FRANK   Well—let's say that it began with eggs. (*He packs away the typewriter*) Anyway, that's most of what happened in France. Anyway, the holiday's over, you're back, even Julia's back.

RITA   Is she? Is it all right?

FRANK   (*putting the typewriter on the window desk and the sheets of poetry in the top left drawer*) Perfect. I get the feeling we shall stay together forever; or until she discovers *oeufs à la crécy*.

RITA   *Oeufs à la crécy*? Does that mean eggs? Trish was goin' on about those; is that all it is, eggs?

FRANK   Trish?

RITA   Trish, me flatmate, Trish. God is it that long since I've seen y', Frank? She moved into the flat with me just before I went to summer school.

FRANK   Ah. Is she a good flatmate?

RITA   She's great. Y' know she's dead classy. Y' know like, she's got taste, y' know like you, Frank, she's just got it. Everything in the flat's dead unpretentious, just books an' plants everywhere. D' y' know somethin', Frank? I'm havin' the time of me life; I am y' know. I even feel—(*moving to the window*)—I feel young, you know like them down there.

FRANK   My dear, twenty-six is hardly old.

RITA   I know that; but I mean, I feel young like them ... I can be young. (*She goes to her bag*) Oh listen—(*she puts the bag on the desk and rummages in it, producing a box*)—I bought y' a present back from London—it isn't much but I thought . . .

She gives him a small box

Here.

FRANK *puts on his glasses, gets the scissors out of the pot on the desk, cuts the string and opens the box to reveal an expensive pen*

RITA See what it says—it's engraved.

FRANK (*reading*) 'Must only be used for poetry. By strictest order—Rita' . . . (*He looks up at her*)

RITA I thought it'd be like a gentle hint.

FRANK Gentle?

RITA Every time y' try an' write a letter or a note with that pen, it won't work; you'll read that inscription an' it'll make you feel dead guilty—cos y' not writing poetry. (*She smiles at him*)

FRANK (*getting up and pecking her on the cheek*) Thank you—Rita. (*He sits down again*)

RITA It's a pleasure. Come on. (*She claps her hands*) What are we doin' this term? Let's do a dead good poet. Come on, let's go an' have the tutorial down there.

FRANK (*appalled*) Down where?

RITA (*getting her bag*) Down there—on the grass—come on.

FRANK On the grass? Nobody sits out there at this time of year.

RITA They do—(*looking out of the window*)—there's some of them out there now.

FRANK Well they'll have wet bums.

RITA What's a wet bum. You can sit on a bench. (*She tries to pull him to his feet*) Come on.

FRANK (*remaining sitting*) Rita, I absolutely protest.

RITA Why?

FRANK Like Dracula, I have an aversion to sunlight.

RITA Tch. (*She sighs*) All right. (*She goes to the window*) Let's open a window.

FRANK If you must open a window then go on, open it. (*He swivels round to watch her*)

RITA (*Struggling to open the window*) It won't bleedin' budge.

FRANK I'm not surprised, my dear. It hasn't been opened for generations.

RITA (*abandoning it*) Tch. Y' need air in here, Frank. The room needs airing. (*She goes and opens the door*)

FRANK This room does not need air, thank you very much.

RITA Course it does. A room is like a plant.

FRANK A room is like a plant?

RITA Yeh, it needs air. (*She goes to her chair by the desk and sits*)

FRANK And water, too, presumably? (*He gets up and closes the door*) If you're going to make an analogy why don't we take it the whole way? Let's get a watering-can and water the carpet; bring in two tons of soil and a bag of fertilizer. Maybe we could take cuttings and germinate other little rooms.

RITA Go way, you're mental you are.

FRANK You said it, distinctly, you said, a room is like a plant.

RITA Well!

There is a pause

FRANK Well what?

RITA Well any analogy will break down eventually.

FRANK Yes. And some will break down sooner than others. (*He smiles, goes to the bookcase* UL *and begins searching among the books*) Look, come on ... A great poet you wanted—well— we have one on the course ...

RITA *sits on the desk watching* FRANK

FRANK I was going to introduce you to him earlier. (*As he rummages a book falls to one side revealing a bottle of whisky which has been hidden behind it*) Now—where is he ...?

RITA *goes over and picks up the whisky bottle from the shelf*

RITA Are you still on this stuff?

FRANK Did I ever say I wasn't?

RITA (*putting the bottle down and moving away*) No. But ...

FRANK But what?

RITA Why d' y' do it when y've got so much goin' for y', Frank?

FRANK It is indeed because I have 'so much goin' for me' that I do it. Life is such a rich and frantic whirl that I need the drink to help me step delicately through it.

RITA It'll kill y', Frank.

FRANK Rita, I thought you weren't interested in reforming me.

RITA I'm not. It's just ...

FRANK What?

RITA Just that I thought you'd started reforming yourself.

FRANK Under your influence?

She shrugs

(*He stops searching and turns to face her*) Yes. But Rita—if I repent and reform, what do I do when your influence is no longer here? What do I do when, in appalling sobriety, I watch you walk away and disappear, my influence gone forever?

RITA Who says I'm gonna disappear?

FRANK Oh you will, Rita. You've got to. (*He turns back to the shelves*)

RITA Why have I got to? This course could go on for years. An' when I've got through this one I might even get into the proper university here.

FRANK And we'll all live happily ever after? Your going is as inevitable as—as ...

RITA *Macbeth*?

FRANK (*smiling*) As tragedy, yes: but it will not be a tragedy, because I shall be glad to see you go.

RITA Tch. Thank you very much. (*After a pause*) Will y' really?

FRANK Be glad to see you go? Well I certainly don't want to see you stay in a room like this for the rest of your life. Now. (*He continues searching for the book*)

RITA (*after a pause*) You can be a real misery sometimes, can't' y'? I was dead happy a minute ago an' then you start an' make me feel like I'm having a bad night in a mortuary.

FRANK *finds the book he has been looking for and moves towards* RITA *with it*

FRANK Well here's something to cheer you up—here's our 'dead good' poet—Blake.

RITA Blake? William Blake?

FRANK The man himself. *You* will understand Blake; they over complicate him, Rita, but you will understand—you'll love the man.

RITA I know.

FRANK What? (*He opens the book*) Look—look—read this ... (*He hands her the book and then goes and sits in the swivel chair*)

RITA *looks at the poem on the page indicated and then looks at* FRANK

RITA (*reciting from memory*)
'O Rose, thou art sick!
The invisible worm
That flies in the night,
In the howling storm,

Has found out thy bed
Of crimson joy:
And his dark secret love
Does thy life destroy.'

FRANK You know it!

RITA (*laughing*) Yeh. (*She tosses the book on the desk and perches on the* UL *bookcase*) We did him at summer school.

FRANK Blake at summer school? You weren't supposed to do Blake at summer school, were you?

RITA Nah. We had this lecturer though, he was a real Blake freak. He was on about it every day. Everythin' he said, honest, everything was related to Blake—he couldn't get his dinner in the refectory without relating it to Blake—Blake and Chips. He was good though. On the last day we brought

55

him a present, an' on it we put that poem, y' know, 'The
Sick Rose'. But we changed it about a bit; it was—erm—

'O Rose, thou aren't sick
Just mangled and dead
Since the rotten gardener
Pruned off thy head.'

We thought he might be narked but he wasn't, he loved it.
He said—what was it ...? He said, 'Parody is merely a
compliment masquerading as humour'.

FRANK (getting up and replacing the book on the shelf) So ...
you've already done Blake? You covered all the Songs of
Innocence and Experience?

RITA Of course; you don't do Blake without doing innocence
and experience, do y'?

FRANK No. Of course. (He goes and sits in the swivel chair)
Black-out

RITA picks up her bag and shawl and exits

Scene two

The lights come up on FRANK who is sitting at his desk marking an
essay. Occasionally he makes a tutting sound and scribbles something.
There is a knock at the door

FRANK Come in.

RITA enters, closes the door, goes to the desk and dumps her bag on it.
She takes her chair and places it next to FRANK and sits down

RITA (talking in a peculiar voice) Hello, Frank.

FRANK (without looking up) Hello. Rita, you're late.

RITA I know, Frank. I'm terribly sorry. It was unavoidable.

FRANK (looking up) Was it really? What's wrong with your
voice?

RITA Nothing is wrong with it, Frank. I have merely decided
to talk properly. As Trish says there is not a lot of point in
discussing beautiful literature in an ugly voice.

56

FRANK You haven't got an ugly voice; at least you *didn't* have. Talk properly.

RITA I am talking properly. I have to practise constantly, in everyday situations.

FRANK You mean you're going to talk like that for the rest of this tutorial?

RITA Trish says that no matter how difficult I may find it I must persevere.

FRANK Well will you kindly tell Trish that I am not giving a tutorial to a Dalek?

RITA I am not a Dalek.

FRANK (*appealingly*) Rita, stop it!

RITA But Frank, I have to persevere in order that I shall.

FRANK Rita! Just be yourself.

RITA (*reverting to her normal voice*) I am being myself. (*She gets up and moves the chair back to its usual place*)

FRANK What's that?

RITA What?

FRANK On your back.

RITA (*reaching up*) Oh—it's grass.

FRANK Grass?

RITA Yeh, I got here early today. I started talking to some students down on the lawn. (*She sits in her usual chair*)

FRANK You were talking to students—down there?

RITA (*laughing*) Don't sound so surprised. I can talk now y' know, Frank.

FRANK I'm not surprised. Well! You used to be quite wary of them didn't you?

RITA God knows why. For students they don't half come out with some rubbish y' know.

FRANK You're telling me?

RITA I only got talking to them in the first place because as I was walking past I heard one of them sayin' as a novel he preferred *Lady Chatterley* to *Sons and Lovers*. I thought, I can keep walkin' and ignore it, or I can put him straight. So I put him straight. I walked over an' said, 'Excuse me but I couldn't help overhearin' the rubbish you were spoutin' about Lawrence'. Shoulda seen the faces on them, Frank. I said tryin' to compare *Chatterley* with *Sons and Lovers* is like tryin' to compare sparkling wine with champagne. The next thing is there's this heated discussion, with me right in the middle of it.

FRANK   I thought you said the student claimed to 'prefer' *Chatterley*, as a novel.

RITA   He did.

FRANK   So he wasn't actually suggesting that it was superior.

RITA   Not at first—but then he did. He walked right into it . . .

FRANK   And so you finished him off, did you, Rita?

RITA   Frank, he was askin' for it. He was an idiot. His argument just crumbled. It wasn't just me—everyone else agreed with me.

FRANK *returns to reading the essay*

RITA   There was this really mad one with them; I've only been talkin' to them for five minutes and he's inviting me to go abroad with them all. They're all goin' to the South of France in the Christmas holidays, slummin' it.

FRANK   You can't go.

RITA   What?

FRANK   You can't go—you've got your exams.

RITA   My exams are before Christmas.

FRANK   Well—you've got your results to wait for . . .

RITA   Tch. I couldn't go anyway.

FRANK   Why? (*He looks at her*)

RITA   It's all right for them. They *can* just jump into a bleedin' van an' go away. But I can't.

He returns to the essay

Tiger they call him, he's the mad one. His real name's Tyson but they call him Tiger.

FRANK   (*looking up*) Is there any point me going on with this? (*He points to the essay*)

RITA What?

FRANK Is there much point in working towards an examination if you're going to fall in love and set off for the South of . . .

RITA (*shocked*) What! Fall in love? With who? My God, Frank, I've just been talkin' to some students. I've heard of match-making but this is ridiculous.

FRANK All right, but please stop burbling on about Mr Tyson.

RITA I haven't been burbling on.

He returns to the essay

What's it like?

FRANK Oh—it—erm—wouldn't look out of place with these. (*He places it on top of a pile of other essays on his desk*)

RITA Honest?

FRANK Dead honest.

Black-out

FRANK *exits*

Scene three

The lights come up on RITA *who is sitting in the armchair by the window, reading a heavy tome. There is the sound of muffled oaths from behind the door*

FRANK *enters carrying his briefcase. He is very drunk*

FRANK Sod them—no, fuck them! Fuck them, eh, Rita? (*He goes to the desk*)

RITA Who?

FRANK You'd tell them wouldn't you? You'd tell them where to get off. (*He gets a bottle of whisky from his briefcase*)

RITA Tell who, Frank?

FRANK Yes—students—students reported me! (*He goes to the*

bookcase UR *and puts the whisky on the shelf*) Me! Complained—
you know something? They complained and it was the best
lecture I've ever given.

RITA   Were you pissed?

FRANK   Pissed? I was glorious! Fell off the rostrum twice. (*He
comes round to the front of his desk*)

RITA   Will they sack you?

FRANK   (*lying flat on the floor*) The sack? God no; that would
involve making a decision. Pissed is all right. To get the sack
it'd have to be rape on a grand scale; and not just the
students either.

RITA *gets up and moves across to look at him*

FRANK   That would only amount to a slight misdemeanour.
For dismissal it'd have to be nothing less than buggering the
bursar ... They suggested a sabbatical for a year—or ten
... Europe—or America ... I suggested that Australia
might be more apt—the allusion was lost on them ...

RITA   Tch. Frank, you're mad.

FRANK   Completely off my cake. I know.

RITA   Even if y' don't think about yourself, what about the
students?

FRANK   *What* about the students?

RITA   Well it's hardly fair on them if their lecturer's so pissed
that he's falling off the rostrum. (*She goes to her chair by the desk
and replaces the book in her bag*)

FRANK   I might have fallen off, my dear, but I went down
talking—and came up talking—never missed a syllable—
what have they got to complain about?

RITA   Maybe they did it for your own good.

FRANK   Or maybe they did it because they're a crowd of
mealy-mouthed pricks who wouldn't know a poet if you
beat them about the head with one. (*He half-sits up*)
'Assonance'—I said to them—'Assonance means getting
the rhyme wrong ...' (*He collapses back on to the floor again*)
They looked at me as though I'd desecrated Wordsworth's
tomb.

RITA Look, Frank, we'll talk about the Blake essay next week, eh?

FRANK Where are you going? We've got a tutorial (*He gets up and staggers towards her*)

RITA Frank, you're not in any fit state for a tutorial. I'll leave it with y' an' we can talk about it next week, eh?

FRANK No—no—you must stay—erm ... Watch this—sober? (*He takes a huge breath and pulls himself together*) Sober! Come on ...

He takes hold of RITA *and pushes her round the desk and sits her in the swivel chair*

You can't go. I want to talk to you about this. (*He gets her essay and shows it to her*) Rita, what's this?

RITA Is there something wrong with it?

FRANK It's just, look, this passage about 'The Blossom' you seem to assume that the poem is about sexuality.

RITA It is!

FRANK Is it?

RITA Well it's certainly a like richer poem, isn't it? If it's interpreted in that way.

FRANK Richer? Why richer? We discussed it. The poem is a simple, uncomplicated piece about blossom, as if seen from a child's point of view.

RITA (*shrugging*) In one sense. But it's like, like the poem about the rose, isn't it? It becomes a more rewarding poem when you see that it works on a number of levels.

FRANK Rita, 'The Blossom' is a simple uncomplicated ...

RITA Yeh, that's what you say, Frank; but Trish and me and some others were talkin' the other night, about Blake, an' what came out of our discussion was that apart from the simple surface value of Blake's poetry there's always a like erm—erm—

FRANK Well? Go on ...

RITA (*managing to*)—a like vein. Of concealed meaning. I mean if that poem's only about the blossom then it's not much of a poem is it?

FRANK   So? You think it gains from being interpreted in this way?

RITA   (*slightly defiantly*) Is me essay wrong then, Frank?

FRANK   It's not—not wrong. But I don't like it.

RITA   You're being subjective.

FRANK   (*half laughing*) Yes—yes I suppose I am. (*He goes slowly to the chair* UC *of the desk and sits down heavily*)

RITA   If it was in an exam what sort of mark would it get?

FRANK   A good one.

RITA   Well what the hell are you sayin' then?

FRANK   (*shrugging*) What I'm saying is that it's up to the minute, quite acceptable, trendy stuff about Blake; but there's nothing of you in there.

RITA   Or maybe Frank, y' mean there's nothing of your views in there.

FRANK   (*after a pause*) Maybe that is what I mean?

RITA   But when I first came to you, Frank, you didn't give me any views. You let me find my own.

FRANK   (*gently*) And your views I still value. But, Rita, these aren't your views.

RITA   But you told me not to have a view. You told me to be objective, to consult recognized authorities. Well that's what I've done; I've talked to other people, read other books an' after consultin' a wide variety of opinion I came up with those conclusions.

He looks at her

FRANK   (*after a pause*) Yes. All right.

RITA   (*rattled*) Look, Frank, I don't have to go along one hundred per cent with your views on Blake y' know. I can have a mind of my own can't I?

FRANK   I sincerely hope so, my dear.

RITA   And what's that supposed to mean?

FRANK   It means—it means be careful.

RITA *jumps up and moves in towards* FRANK

RITA   (*angrily*) What d' y' mean be careful? I can look after myself. Just cos I'm learnin', just cos I can do it now an'

read what I wanna read an' understand without havin' to
come runnin' to you every five minutes y' start tellin' me to
be careful. (*She paces about*)

FRANK Because—because *I* care for you—I want you to care
for yourself.

RITA Tch. (*She goes right up to* FRANK. *After a pause*) I—I care
for you, Frank ... But you've got to—to leave me alone a
bit. I'm not an idiot now, Frank—I don't need you to hold
me hand as much ... I can—I can do things on me own
more now ... And I am careful. I know what I'm doin'. Just
don't—don't keep treatin' me as though I'm the same as
when I first walked in here. I understand now, Frank; I
know the difference between—between—Somerset Maugham an' Harold Robbins. An' you're still treating me as
though I'm hung up on *Rubyfruit Jungle*. (*She goes to the swivel
chair and sits*) Just ... You understand, don't you Frank?

FRANK Entirely, my dear.

RITA I'm sorry.

FRANK Not at all. (*After a pause*) I got around to reading it
you know, *Rubyfruit Jungle*. It's excellent.

RITA (*laughing*) Oh go way, Frank. Of its type it's quite
interesting. But it's hardly excellence.

Black-out

RITA *exits*

Scene four

The lights come up on FRANK *sitting in the swivel chair*
RITA *enters and goes to the desk*

RITA Frank ...
He looks at his watch
  I know I'm late ... I'm sorry.
He gets up and moves away
  Am I too late? We were talkin'. I didn't notice the time.

FRANK   Talking?

RITA   Yeh. If it'll go in my favour we were talking about Shakespeare.

FRANK   Yes ... I'm sure you were.

RITA   Am I too late then? All right. I'll be on time next week. I promise.

FRANK   Rita. Don't go.

RITA   No—honestly, Frank—I know I've wasted your time. I'll see y' next week, eh?

FRANK   Rita! Sit down!

RITA *goes to her usual chair and sits*

FRANK   (*Going to the side of her*) When you were so late I phoned the shop.

RITA   Which shop?

FRANK   The hairdresser's shop. Where you work. Or, I should say, worked.

RITA   I haven't worked there for a long time. I work in a bistro now.

FRANK   You didn't tell me.

RITA   Didn't I? I thought I did. I was telling someone.

FRANK   It wasn't me.

RITA   Oh. Sorry. (*After a pause*) What's wrong?

FRANK   (*after a pause*) It struck me that there was a time when you told me everything.

RITA   I thought I had told you.

FRANK   No. Like a drink?

RITA   Who cares if I've left hairdressin' to work in a bistro?

FRANK   I care. (*He goes* UR *to the bookshelves and takes a bottle from an eye-level shelf*) You don't want a drink? Mind if I do?

RITA   But why do you care about details like that? It's just boring, insignificant detail.

FRANK   (*getting a mug from the small table*) Oh. Is it?

RITA   That's why I couldn't stand being in a hairdresser's any longer; boring irrelevant detail all the time, on and on ... Well I'm sorry but I've had enough of that. I don't wanna talk about irrelevant rubbish anymore.

FRANK   And what do you talk about in your bistro? Cheers.

RITA   Everything.

FRANK   Everything?

RITA   Yeh.

FRANK   Ah.

RITA   We talk about what's important, Frank, and we leave out the boring details for those who want them.

FRANK   Is Mr Tyson one of your customers?

RITA   A lot of students come in; he's one of them. You're not gonna give me another warning are y', Frank?

FRANK   Would it do any good?

RITA   Look, for your information I do find Tiger fascinatin', like I find a lot of the people I mix with fascinating; they're young, and they're passionate about things that matter. They're not trapped—they're too young for that. And I like to be with them.

FRANK   (*moving* DR *of the desk and keeping his back to her*) Perhaps —perhaps you don't want to waste your time coming here anymore?

RITA   Don't be stupid. I'm sorry I was late. (*After a pause she gets up*) Look, Frank, I've got to go. I'm meeting Trish at seven. We're going to see a production of *The Seagull*.

FRANK   Yes. (*He turns to face her*) Well. When Chekhov calls . . .

RITA   Tch.

FRANK   You can hardly bear to spend a moment here can you?

RITA   (*moving towards him a little*) That isn't true. It's just that I've got to go to the theatre.

FRANK   And last week you didn't turn up at all. Just a phone call to say you had to cancel.

RITA   It's just that—that there's so many things happening now. It's harder.

FRANK   As I said, Rita, if you want to stop com—

RITA   (*going right up to him*) For God's sake, I don't want to stop coming here. I've got to come here. What about my exam?

65

FRANK   Oh I wouldn't worry about that. You'd sail through it anyway. You really don't have to put in the odd appearance out of sentimentality; (*he moves round to the other side of the desk*) I'd rather you spared me that.

FRANK *goes to drink*

RITA   If you could stop pouring that junk down your throat in the hope that it'll make you feel like a poet you might be able to talk about things that matter instead of where I do or don't work; an' then it might be worth comin' here.

FRANK   Are you capable of recognizing what does or does not matter, Rita?

RITA   I understand literary criticism, Frank. When I come here that's what we're supposed to be dealing with.

FRANK   You want literary criticism? (*He looks at her for a moment and then goes to the top drawer of his desk and takes out two slim volumes and some typewritten sheets of poetry and hands them to her*) I want an essay on that lot by next week.

RITA   What is it?

FRANK   No sentimentality, no subjectivity. Just pure criticism. A critical assessment of a lesser known English poet. Me.

Black-out

RITA *exits*

Scene five

The lights come up on FRANK *sitting in a chair by the window desk with a mug in his hand and a bottle of whisky on the desk in front of him listening to the radio. There is a knock at the door*

FRANK   Come in.

RITA *enters and goes to the swivel chair behind Frank's desk*

FRANK   (*Getting up and switching off the radio*) What the—what the hell are you doing here? I'm not seeing you till next week.

RITA   Are you sober? Are you?

FRANK   If you mean am I still this side of reasonable comprehension, then yes.

RITA   (*going and standing next to him*) Because I want you to hear this when you're sober. (*She produces his poems*) These are brilliant. Frank, you've got to start writing again. (*She goes to the swivel chair and sits*) This is brilliant. They're witty. They're profound. Full of style.

FRANK   (*going to the small table and putting down his mug*) Ah ... tell me again, and again ...

RITA   They are, Frank. It isn't only me who thinks so. Me an' Trish sat up last night and read them. She agrees with me. Why did you stop writing? Why did you stop when you can produce work like this? We stayed up most of the night, just talking about it. At first we just saw it as contemporary poetry in its own right, you know, as somethin' particular to this century but look, Frank, what makes it more—more ... What did Trish say—? More resonant than—purely contemporary poetry in that you can see in it a direct line through to nineteenth-century traditions of—of like wit an' classical allusion.

FRANK   (*going to the chair U of the desk and standing by the side of it*) Er—that's erm—that's marvellous, Rita. How fortunate I didn't let you see it earlier. Just think if I'd let you see it when you first came here.

RITA   I know ... I wouldn't have understood it, Frank.

FRANK   You would have thrown it across the room and dismissed it as a heap of shit, wouldn't you?

RITA   (*laughing*) I know ... But I couldn't have understood it then, Frank, because I wouldn't have been able to recognize and understand the allusions.

FRANK   Oh I've done a fine job on you, haven't I.

RITA   It's true, Frank. I can see now.

FRANK   You know, Rita, I think—I think that like you I shall change my name; from now on I shall insist upon being known as Mary, Mary Shelley—do you understand that allusion, Rita?

RITA What?

FRANK She wrote a little Gothic number called *Frankenstein*.

RITA So?

FRANK This—(*picking up his poetry and moving round to* RITA)—this clever, pyrotechnical pile of self-conscious allusion is worthless, talentless, shit and could be recognized as such by anyone with a shred of common sense. It's the sort of thing that gives publishing a bad name. Wit? You'll find more wit in the telephone book, and, probably, more insight. Its one advantage over the telephone directory is that it's easier to rip. (*He rips the poems up and throws the pieces on to the desk*) It is pretentious, characterless and without style.

RITA It's not.

FRANK Oh, I don't expect you to believe me, Rita; you recognize the hallmark of literature now, don't you? (*In a final gesture he throws a handful of the ripped pieces into the air and then goes to the chair* DR *and sits*) Why don't you just go away? I don't think I can bear it any longer.

RITA Can't bear what, Frank?

FRANK You, my dear—you ...

RITA I'll tell you what you can't bear, Mr Self-Pitying Piss Artist; what you can't bear is that I am educated now. What's up, Frank, don't y' like me now that the little girl's grown up, now that y' can no longer bounce me on daddy's knee an' watch me stare back in wide-eyed wonder at everything he has to say? I'm educated, I've got what you have an' y' don't like it because you'd rather see me as the peasant I once was; you're like the rest of them—you like to keep your natives thick, because that way they still look charming and delightful. I don't need you. (*She gets up and picking up her bag moves away from the desk in the direction of the door*) I've got a room full of books. I know what clothes to wear, what wine to buy, what plays to see, what papers and books to read. I can do without you.

FRANK   Is that all you wanted. Have you come all this way for so very, very little?

RITA   Oh it's little to you, isn't it? It's little to you who squanders every opportunity and mocks and takes it for granted.

FRANK   Found a culture have you, Rita? Found a better song to sing have you? No—you've found a different song, that's all—and on your lips it's shrill and hollow and tuneless. Oh, Rita, Rita . . .

RITA   Rita? (*She laughs*) Rita? Nobody calls me Rita but you. I dropped that pretentious crap as soon as I saw it for what it was. You stupid . . . Nobody calls me Rita.

FRANK   What is it now then? Virginia?

RITA *exits*

FRANK   Or Charlotte? Or Jane? Or Emily?

Black-out

Scene Six

The lights come up on FRANK *talking into the telephone. He is leaning against the bookshelf.*

FRANK   Yes . . . I think she works there . . . Rita White . . . No, no. Sorry . . . erm. What is it? . . . Susan White? No? . . . Thank you . . . Thanks . . .

The lights fade to black-out to denote the passing of some time and then come up on FRANK *sitting at his desk with his back to the audience. He is drunk and talking on the telephone*

Yes . . . Erm . . . Trish is it? . . . Erm, yes I'm a friend of Rita's . . . Rita . . . I'm sorry Susan . . . yes . . . could you just say that—erm— I've . . . it's—erm—Frank here . . . her tutor . . . Yes . . . well could you tell her that I have—erm—I've entered her for her examination . . . Yes you see she doesn't know the details . . . time and where the exam is being held

... Could you tell her to call in? ... Please ... Yes ... Thank you.

The lights fade to black-out

Scene seven

The lights come up

RITA *enters and shuts the door. She is wrapped in a large winter coat. She lights a cigarette and moves across to the filing cabinet and places a Christmas card with the others already there. She throws the envelope in the waste-bin and opens the door revealing* FRANK *with a couple of tea-chests either side of him. He is taken aback at seeing her and then he gathers himself and, picking up one of the chests, enters the room.* RITA *goes out to the corridor and brings in the other chest.*

FRANK *gets the chair from the* U *end of his desk and places it by the* UL *bookcase. He stands on it and begins taking down the books from the shelves and putting them into the chests.* RITA *watches him but he continues as if she is not there*

RITA Merry Christmas, Frank. Have they sacked y'?

FRANK Not quite.

RITA Well, why y'—packing your books away?

FRANK Australia. (*After a pause*) Some weeks ago—made rather a night of it.

RITA Did y' bugger the bursar?

FRANK Metaphorically. And as it was metaphorical the sentence was reduced from the sack to two years in Australia. Hardly a reduction in sentence really—but ...

RITA What y' gonna do?

FRANK *Bon voyage.*

RITA She's not goin' with y'?

FRANK *shakes his head.* RITA *begins helping him take down the books from the shelves and putting them in the chests*

70

RITA   What y' gonna do?

FRANK   What do you think I'll do? Aussie? It's a paradise for the likes of me.

RITA   Tch. Come on, Frank . . .

FRANK   It is, Didn't you know the Australians named their favourite drink after a literary figure? Forster's Lager they call it. Of course they get the spelling wrong—rather like you once did!

RITA   Be serious.

FRANK   For God's sake, why did you come back here?

RITA   I came to tell you you're a good teacher. (*After a pause*) Thanks for enterin' me for the exam.

FRANK   That's all right. I know how much it had come to mean to you.

RITA *perches on the small table while* FRANK *continues to take books from the upper shelves*

RITA   You didn't want me to take it, did y'? Eh? You woulda loved it if I'd written, 'Frank knows all the answers', across me paper, wouldn't y'? I nearly did an' all. When the invigilator said, 'Begin', I turned over me paper with the rest of them, and while they were all scribbling away against the clock, I just sat there, lookin' at the first question. Y' know what it was, Frank? 'Suggest ways in which one might cope with some of the staging difficulties in a production of *Peer Gynt.*'

FRANK *gets down, sits on the chair and continues to pack the books*

FRANK   Well, you should have had no trouble with that.

RITA   I did though. I just sat lookin' at the paper an' thinkin' about what you'd said. I tried to ignore it, to pretend that you were wrong. You think you gave me nothing; did nothing for me. You think I just ended up with a load of quotes an' empty phrases; an' I did. But that wasn't your doin'. I was so hungry. I wanted it all so much that I didn't want it to be questioned. I told y' I was stupid. It's like Trish, y' know me flatmate, I thought she was so cool an' together—I came home the other night an' she'd

71

tried to top herself. Magic, isn't it? She spends half her life eatin' wholefoods an' health foods to make her live longer, an' the other half tryin' to kill herself. (*After a pause*) I sat lookin' at the question, an' thinkin' about it all. Then I picked up me pen an' started.

FRANK   And you wrote, 'Do it on the radio'?

RITA   I could have done. An' you'd have been proud of me if I'd done that an' rushed back to tell you—wouldn't y'? But I chose not to. I had a choice. I did the exam.

FRANK   I know. A good pass as well.

RITA   Yeh. An' it might be worthless in the end. But I had a choice. I chose, me. Because of what you'd given me I had a choice. I wanted to come back an' tell y' that. That y' a good teacher.

FRANK   (*stopping working and looking at her*) You know—erm—I hear very good things about Australia. Things are just beginning there. The thing is, why don't you—come as well? It'd be good for us to leave a place that's just finishing for one that's just beginning.

RITA   Isn't that called jumpin' a sinkin' ship?

FRANK   So what? Do you really think there's any chance of us keeping it afloat?

She looks at him and then at the shelves

RITA   (*seeing the empty whisky bottles*) 'Ey, Frank, if there was threepence back on each of those bottles you could buy Australia.

FRANK   (*smiling*) You're being evasive.

RITA   (*going and sitting on a tea-chest*) I know. Tiger's asked me to go down to France with his mob.

FRANK   Will you?

RITA   I dunno. He's a bit of a wanker really. But I've never been abroad. An' me mother's invited me to her's for Christmas.

FRANK   What are you going to do?

RITA   I dunno. I might go to France. I might go to me

mother's. I might even have a baby. I dunno. I'll make a decision, I'll chose. I dunno.

FRANK *has found a package hidden behind some of the books. He takes it down*

FRANK   Whatever you do, you might as well take this ...

RITA   What?

FRANK   (*handing it to her*) It's erm—well, it's er—it's a dress really. I bought it some time ago—for erm—for an educated woman friend—of mine ...

RITA *takes the dress from the bag*

FRANK   I erm—don't—know if it fits, I was rather pissed when I bought it ...

RITA   An educated woman, Frank? An' is this what you call a scholarly neckline?

FRANK   When choosing it I put rather more emphasis on the word woman than the word educated.

RITA   All I've ever done is take from you I've never given anything.

FRANK   That's not true you've ...

RITA   It is true. I never thought there was anythin' I could give you. But there is. Come here, Frank ...

FRANK   What?

RITA   Come here ... (*She pulls out a chair*) Sit on that ...

FRANK *is bewildered*

RITA   Sit ...

FRANK *sits and* RITA, *eventually finding a pair of scissors on the desk, waves them in the air*

RITA   I'm gonna take ten years off you ...

She goes across to him and begins to cut his hair. As she gets close to his ear-lobe FRANK *cries out 'Ouch'*

Black-out

Notes

The notes in this edition are intended to serve the needs of overseas students as well as those of British-born users.

Inverted commas indicate references to stage directions.

Act One

Scene one

1 *Eliot*: T S Eliot (1888–1965), American-born British poet, critic and dramatist. Widely regarded as one of the most influential writers and thinkers of the twentieth century.

Dickens: Charles Dickens (1812–70), English novelist noted for the vitality of his writing and the memorability of his characters. Author of such classics as *Oliver Twist*, *Great Expectations* and *Bleak House*.

'*slug*': measure (of alcohol).

'*shifts a lot of booze*': consumes a good deal of drink.

Open University: British university system by means of which students of all ages can enrol to study on a part-time basis instead of attending full-time courses at one of the more traditional universities. Lectures are broadcast on radio and television, while tutorials and classes are conducted by teachers attached to established colleges and universities. Open University degrees are awarded to students on successful completion of their courses.

2 *Henry James*: (1843–1916), American novelist who later in life settled in England. His main contribution has been in the area of the psychological novel, plot being subordinated to detailed examination of characters and the recounting of apparently insignificant incidents. His best

works include *Portrait of a Lady, What Maisie Knew* and *The Ambassadors*.

ratatouille: vegetable stew made up of onions, aubergines, courgettes and tomatoes which have been cooked slowly together.

put your head in the oven: putting one's head in an unlit oven and inhaling the coal-gas was a not uncommon means of committing suicide in the days before the introduction of natural gas.

bleedin': swear-word denoting irritation. Rita swears profusely in the course of the play; her doing so is an essential part of her personality. She swears unthinkingly and seldom with any real force, unaware of the actual meaning of the words she uses. See her discussion of the topic with Frank on page 6. In the notes which follow, explanations of her obscene language will only be given where a particular meaning is intended.

sod (obscene): fellow, person.

3 *tits*: breasts.

'*Men Only*': popular magazine containing glossy photographs of nude and near-nude women.

4 *inflation*: rise in the cost of living.

more comprehensive studentship: students drawn from a wider range of ability and background than is normally the case at more conventional universities. See also note to *Open University*, page 1.

'*Brownie salute*': the Brownies, a junior branch of the Girl Guide organization, aims to teach its members such qualities as honesty, reliability and kindness. Rita jokingly gives the Brownie salute as a sign that she means to keep her promise not to tell about Frank's smoking.

5 *I read . . . Thomas*: Dylan Thomas (1914–53) was a highly gifted Welsh poet. One of his most powerful poems is entitled 'Do not go gentle into that good night'. In it he urges his dying father not to give in to death, but to fight against it to the bitter end.

Roger McGough: popular English poet, born in Liverpool, who first came to prominence in the 1960s, at the same time as the Beatles (see also Willy Russell's personal essay, page x).

pissed (obscene): drunk.

dead (colloquial): very, really.

Scotch: whisky distilled in Scotland.

'*Howard's End*': novel by E M Forster (see note below) first published in 1910.

It sounds filthy: Rita is alluding to the phrase 'getting your end away' a euphemism for sexual intercourse.

E. M. Forster: (1879–1970) English writer, distinguished author of a relatively small number of novels, of which the most celebrated is *A Passage to India*. Frank remembers Rita's confusion of 'Forster' and 'Foster' as he packs his books in Act Two, scene seven—see note to *Forster's Lager*, page 71.

pack the course in: give (it) up.

6 *soft* (colloquial): silly.

telly (colloquial): television.

fuckin': swear word used simply to add force to what the speaker is saying.

fucked (obscene): tired, worn out.

7 *effin' and blindin'*: swearing.

fackin': Rita's imitation of upper-class pronunciation.

round our way: in the place where I live (meaning here among people of Rita's background).

collect a gold star: it was common in schools at one time to award gold star-shaped badges to clever or hardworking pupils, who wore them as a sign of their achievement.

8 *assonance*: the repetition of similar vowel sounds, usually close together, in order to create a harmonious effect. Frank gives an example a few lines later.

Yeats: W B Yeats (1865–1939), Irish poet and dramatist particularly associated with the revival of Irish culture towards the end of the nineteenth century.

wine lodge: a chain of bars in the North called 'Yates's Wine Lodges' which specialize in selling Australian white wine. Rita thinks that when Frank mentions 'Yeats', he is referring to these bars.

loads: much, a lot.

9 *Rita Mae Brown*: American writer of popular fiction.

'Rubyfruit Jungle': novel by Rita Mae Brown dealing in explicit terms with relationships between women.

lend: Rita makes a common mistake: she means to say 'borrow'.

'blurb': publisher's description of the contents of a book, usually 'selling' it by emphasizing its good qualities.

Frank Harris: (1856–1931) British writer and journalist whose best-known work, *Life and Loves*, was banned as pornographic by the authorities. It is ironic that he is the only writer that Rita knows much about at this stage in her education.

the quality: the best people, someone really distinguished.

copper (colloquial): policeman.

Al Capone: infamous American gangster and racketeer of the 1920s.

T. S. Eliot: see note to page 1

9–10 *J. Arthur Prufrock ... something else altogether*: one of T S Eliot's best-known poems is entitled 'The Love Song of J. Alfred Prufrock'. Rita confuses the hero of this work with the well-known British film-maker and industrialist, J Arthur Rank (later Lord Rank), whose name is often used as a rhyming slang euphemism for the word 'wank', itself a euphemistic obscenity meaning masturbation.

doin' a perm: putting a 'permanent' wave in a customer's hair.

10 *Farrah Fawcett Majors*: American film and television actress of the 1970s and '80s, noted for her striking hair style. Most popular among British viewers for her role in the television series *Charlie's Angels*.

11 *ITV*: the independent television network in Britain.

BBC: the British Broadcasting Corporation—the state-owned radio and television company.

Flora: popular brand of margarine, widely advertised as being good for people because low in cholesterol, a chemical which in excessive quantities encourages heart disease. In the early 1980s, a series of television advertisements suggested that it would be a good idea for wives to persuade their husbands to eat Flora rather than butter or any other margarine, thus changing them into 'Flora men'.

Flowers: 'flora' is the Latin word for 'flowers'. It is typical of Frank that his mind turns to this classical reference rather than the modern advertising association.

pebble-dashed bread: Rita's name for brown bread containing whole wheat grains and regarded as having higher dietary value than white bread. Pebble-dashing is the method by which the outside walls of buildings may be covered with a rough plaster containing a high percentage of small pebbles. To Rita the grains in the bread are as the pebbles in the mortar.

take the piss (obscene): poke fun, make jokes of things.

12 *Come off the pill*: stop taking an oral contraceptive.

mental: mad, mentally deranged.

narked (colloquial): annoyed.

Formby: coastal town north of Liverpool.

hole: unpleasant, ugly place to live in.

13 *Guinness*: dark-coloured stout, an alcoholic drink originally brewed in Ireland.

as witty as Wilde: Oscar Wilde (1854–1900), the Irish poet, essayist and dramatist, was particularly noted for his quickness of wit and his ability to manipulate words and ideas.

14 *piss artist* (obscene): heavy drinker.

geriatric hippie: the hippies were mainly young, long-haired, drug-taking, peace-loving people who decided to opt out of the high-pressure, materialistic life of the 1950s and '60s, especially in America. Rita suggests that, with his long hair, Frank looks like a hippie who has grown grotesquely old.

Scene two

15 *patina*: strictly speaking, the film that develops on wood or stone over a period of time. Frank applies the term to the state of organized chaos which has developed in his study.

16 *public school*: in the United Kingdom, a private or independent school (as opposed to one that is state-maintained). In general, substantial fees are paid for education at such schools and they tend to be regarded as the special domain of the upper classes.

tuck-shop: school shop catering for the needs of pupils at a public school.

matron: member of staff (usually a trained nurse) employed to be responsible for the health and general welfare of pupils.

prep: short for 'preparation', the boarding-school equivalent of homework, work done of an evening by pupils in preparation for their classes the next day.

minor ... major: it was (and sometimes still is) the custom in some schools to refer to pupils by their surnames (family names) only. In order to overcome the difficulty of indicating which of two brothers with the same surname was being referred to, the practice evolved of calling the younger '... minor' and the older '... major'.

off me cake: crazy, mad. Rita explains, using her own terms 'Soft ... mental' in her next speech.

Isabel Archer: the heroine of the novel *The Portrait of a Lady* by Henry James. See note to page 2.

masochism: the term is used loosely of the morbid acceptance or even enjoyment of pain, whether physical or mental. The notion of applying it to Isabel Archer no doubt springs from the way in which, in James's novel, she forces herself to suffer the enduring misery of an unhappy marriage to a selfish and heartless man, even though opportunities arise for her to free herself from him.

17 *slummin' it* (colloquial): behaving in a fashion inappropriate to (your) education.

the whimps: feeble people, 'wets'.

this livin' lark (colloquial): life.

18 *Jane Austen*: (1775–1817) English novelist, whose books —like *Emma* and *Pride and Prejudice*—are noted for their witty description of middle-class life and manners at the beginning of the nineteenth century.

Tracy Austin: young contemporary American tennis star.

Crap (obscene): rubbish.

established literary critique: body of literary criticism that has been built up over past centuries.

partisan: based on blind or unreasoning prejudice.

F. R. Leavis: distinguished and highly influential contemporary literary critic.

louse (colloquial): person worthy of contempt.

19 *in his ivory tower*: the image of an artist (whether writer or painter or musician) living in an ivory tower is commonly used to suggest his or her remoteness from the concerns of everyday life.

from a Marxist viewpoint: by applying the ideas of Karl Marx (1818–83) the German founder of international communism.

immoral: wicked

Amoral: lying outside considerations of what is right or wrong.

23 *sod of* (obscene): shut up (indicating disbelief in what Frank has just said).

Does ... electrician?: Forster uses the phrase 'only connect' to mean that the most important thing in life is to open

your heart and soul to another human being. Rita jokingly applies it to an electrician 'connecting' or wiring up a
plug.

Scene three

(Willy Russell has suggested that this scene may be
omitted in performance.)

24 *'flounces'*: walks in an abrupt, impatient fashion.

get on my tits (obscene): annoy me—but Frank takes her
words literally ...

it's cutting ... done it: consumption of alcohol raises sexual
desire but reduces the likelihood of its being put into
actual performance. Frank wickedly suggests that his
cutting down on the 'booze' has led to an increased
interest in Rita's physical charms.

Harold Robbins: American writer of popular or pulp fiction—not very highly regarded by serious literary critics.

bring in: introduce (into the essay).

'A Stone for Danny Fisher': novel by Harold Robbins.

prime: wonderful, fine (used here ironically).

25 *'Sons and Lovers'*: important semi-autobiographical novel
by the English novelist D H Lawrence (1895–1930).

Noël Coward: (1899–1973) English dramatist, actor and
composer noted particularly for his satire and witty dialogue.

Somerset Maugham: (1874–1965) British novelist and
short-story writer. *Of Human Bondage*, an autobio-
graphical work, is widely regarded as his masterpiece.

perverted: Rita associates the word 'bondage' with the
performance of certain unorthodox sexual practices, involving the tying up and beating of one partner by the
other.

posher: of better social class.

26 *have a bit of slap an' tickle*: Rita equates reading pulp

fiction (which should not be introduced into serious essays) with indulging in light-hearted sexual flirtation (which—because it is not serious—should not be confessed to one's family).

Scene four

'Peer Gynt': large-scale dramatic poem by the Norwegian poet and dramatist, Henrik Ibsen (1828–1906).

27 *as thin as this*: as lacking in critical substance and depth as this.

encapsulated: condensed.

29 *thick* (colloquial): stupid.

30 *on the Valium*: taking Valium, a type of tranquillizing drug.

keg beer: beer stored under pressure in and sold from strongly built metal containers or 'kegs'. Regarded by many as being inferior to beer brewed and stored in wooden barrels in the traditional fashion.

'Daily Mirror' ... the *'Sun'*: popular national newspapers in Britain, published daily.

31 *an'* ... *connect*: see note to *does* ... *electrician?*, page 23 .

Scene five

32 *Chekhov*: Anton Chekhov (1860–1904), Russian author and dramatist—perhaps the most popular Russian writer outside his own country.

prescription: direction for the preparation of a medicine (in this case the contraceptive pill) written by a doctor and given to his patient to have made up by a chemist.

33 *y' soft get* (colloquial): you stupid fool.

havin' it off (colloquial): having a sexual affair.

shack up with (colloquial): move in with, live with (without being married).

There's ... milk: (English proverb) nothing can be done about what has already happened, so there's no point in worrying about it.

34 *rockin' the coffin* (colloquial): disturbing the pattern of life (or—as she sees it—death) that he wants Rita to follow.

lager: light-coloured bitter beer.

Everton ... Liverpool: professional football teams based in the Liverpool area.

the dole: state payment made to those who are unemployed.

Stork: popular brand of margarine, whose taste is advertised as being indistinguishable from that of butter.

pots: glasses, tankards.

35 *stashed* (colloquial): hidden away.

36 *that Chekhov play ... at him?*: the play in question is Chekhov's *The Seagull* (see note below).

Does he go?: Rita takes Frank to be asking whether or not she has ever seen Chekhov in person at a theatre.

deaf and dumb breakfasts: breakfasts at which there will be a tense silence between Frank and Julia.

37 *an M. A.*: degree of Master of Arts.

The Seagull: first produced in 1896, one of Chekhov's best-known plays.

The Importance ... Thingy: Rita can't quite get the name of the play right: she is referring to Oscar Wilde's comic masterpiece, *The Importance of Being Earnest*. See also note to *as witty as Wilde*, page 13.

'(aghast)' An amateur production?: Frank's outburst derives from his sharing of the commonly held opinion that performances of plays by unpaid amateur actors are bound to be in some way inferior to those in which professional actors take part.

38 *there's no ... tonight*: Frank anticipates that the amateur production will be lifelessly and woodenly acted.

Y've gorra (dialect): you've got to.

Scene six

39 *Shakespeare*: William Shakespeare (1564–1616), England's greatest poet and dramatist: his works are read and studied, both in the original and in translation, all over the world.

it done me in (colloquial): it destroyed me—in the sense of leaving her speechless and numbed by the sheer power of the performance.

Out, out ... nothing: see Shakespeare's *Macbeth*, Act V, scene 5, lines 23–8.

'Romeo and Juliet': another of Shakespeare's plays—Frank deliberately pretends he thinks the quotation comes from *Romeo and Juliet* in order to tease (and perhaps test) Rita.

40 *cow* (obscene): unpleasant woman.

42 *demi-wave*: light wave or body wave giving straight, fine hair the appearance of greater thickness.

muppet: rag doll, one with wildly untidy hair.

Scene seven

43 *vino* (Italian): wine.

stage-manager type: a stage-manager in a theatre is the man or woman responsible for the smooth running of a performance, ensuring props and scenery are in position, lighting and sound are cued correctly and actors and actresses make their entrances at the right moments. Julia clearly likes to run her dinner parties in a similarly highly organized way.

yours: your house.

44 *Shaw*: George Bernard Shaw (1856–1950), eminent Irish-born critic, dramatist and man of ideas. *Shavian* is the adjective derived from his surname; it is often used with reference to the characteristic blend of humour and seriousness to be found in his plays.

plonk: cheap wine.

breezed in: entered in a carefree manner.

45 *to play the court jester*: to be laughed at by the people present.

analyst: psychoanalyst.

paranoia: mental illness in which the sufferer has a fixed delusion about him- or herself: for instance, of inferiority to others or that other people are persecuting him in some way.

half-caste: in the sense of not properly belonging either to the sort of people among whom she has grown up or to those with whom Frank mixes.

our Sandra: my sister Sandra.

mates: friends.

Scene eight

46 *ultimatum*: final demand.

narked (colloquial): annoyed, angry.

47 *warped*: distorted, corrupted.

48 *dump*: throw.

Act Two

Scene one

49 *Lashin' us*: in the sense of driving (and beating) them as if they were slaves.

50 *Ferlinghetti*: Lawrence Ferlinghetti, contemporary American poet.

Only ... cheese: Rita's wicked sense of humour almost prompts her to reply as if she thinks 'Ferlinghetti' is some kind of Italian pasta dish (like spaghetti or macaroni), usually served with a sprinkling of Parmesan cheese (from Parma, a town in northern Italy) on top.

'Gauloise': brand of French cigarette.

51 *'oeufs en cocotte'*: eggs poached in the oven and served with hot cream.

Florentine, Benedict: methods of serving soft-boiled eggs, the former using a base of spinach, the latter thin slices of ham.

'oeufs à la crécy': poached eggs served with carrots and a cheese sauce.

52 *bums*: backsides.

Like Dracula ... sunlight: most legends associated with the vampire Count Dracula suggest that he avoids the light of day and especially strong sunlight.

53 *budge*: move.

make an analogy: draw a parallel.

55 *William Blake*: (1757–1827) English poet, painter and engraver. Frank suggests that Rita will 'understand' and 'love' his work because of her uncomplicated, childlike approach to literature. Indeed, his *Songs of Innocence*, with their simple language, were specifically designed to be accessible to children as well as adults.

O Rose, thou art sick!: one of the poems in Blake's collection *Songs of Experience*.

freak: fanatic.

refectory: dining-hall.

56 *Parody*: piece of writing in which one author imitates the style, ideas or tone of another, often for humourous effect.

Scene two

57 *Dalek*: alien, robot-like creature featured in the British television series *Dr Who* and noted for its mechanical mode of speech.

'Lady Chatterley' ... *'Sons and Lovers'*: See also note to *Sons and Lovers*, page 25; *Lady Chatterley's Lover* is another of Lawrence's novels—generally considered inferior to *Sons and Lovers* but famous for its explicit sexual detail.

58 *spoutin'* (colloquial): talking in a gushing manner.
59 *burbling on*: talking endlessly.

Scene three

    'tome': book, volume.
60 *rostrum*: raised dais from which Frank had been delivering his lecture.
    sack: dismiss.
    buggering the bursar: committing the act of sodomy with the university's financial officer.
    sabbatical: period of paid study leave.
    mealy-mouthed: smooth-talking, squeamish about saying things too harshly or directly.
    pricks: obscene expression of contempt.
    Assonance: See note to page 8.
    desecrated: done something to Wordsworth's tomb showing disrespect for it.
    Wordsworth: William Wordworth (1770–1850), celebrated English poet and central figure in the so-called Romantic Movement.
61 *'The Blossom'*: one of Blake's *Songs of Innocence* (see note to *William Blake*, page 55).
64 *bistro*: small restaurant.
65 *They're not trapped*: in the sense that they are still sufficiently young to think and behave as they like, without being stuck in a social or professional rut.
    'The Seagull': see note to page 37.

Scene five

67 *still this side of reasonable comprehension*: still sufficiently sober to be reasonably easily understood.
    resonant: resounding, having overtones which chime in the reader's mind.

wit: defined by the poet Alexander Pope (1688–1744) as 'What oft was thought, but ne'er so well expressed'.

classical allusion: quality which enriches a work and gives it depth by association with the best writers of the past.

shit (obscene): rubbish.

68 *Mary Shelley*: (1797–1851) second wife of the poet Shelley and a novelist in her own right. *Frankenstein* (1818) tells the familiar story of the scientist who 'creates' a human being and brings it to life. His problem is that he is unable to control his monstrous creation.

Gothic: Gothic novels were particularly popular in the late eighteenth and early nineteenth centuries. They were usually stories of terror and mystery, involving haunted castles and inexplicable happenings.

number (colloquial): item, (in this case) book.

pyrotechnical: outwardly showy, like fireworks.

Mr Self-Pitying Piss Artist: see note to *piss artist*, page 14.

peasant (colloquial): uneducated person.

69 *Virginia ... Charlotte ... Jane ... Emily*: Frank cruelly suggests that now that she has become educated (as she puts it) Rita will want to change her name to that of one of the great women writers of English literature, such as Virginia Woolf (1882–1941), Charlotte Brontë (1816–55), Jane Austen (1775–1817) or Emily Brontë (1818–48).

Scene seven

70 *'tea-chests'*: wooden boxes used for packing books and other small objects when moving house.

'Bon voyage' (French): have a good (safe) journey.

71 *Aussie*: Australia.

Forster's Lager: see also note to *E. M. Forster*, page 5. Frank deliberately confuses 'Forster' with 'Foster' as Rita did earlier. Foster's Lager is a well-known brand of Australian beer.

invigilator: supervisor at an examination.

72 *top herself* (slang): hang herself, commit suicide.

jumpin' a sinkin' ship: leaving a sinking ship, getting out of a place or situation that is becoming worse and worse.

wanker (obscene): masturbator—one who is primarily concerned with himself.

73 *take ten years off you*: make you look ten years younger.

Study questions

Questions for class discussion

Literature

1   RITA You probably won't think it's any good.
      FRANK Why?
      RITA It's the sort of poetry you can understand.
      FRANK Ah. I see.

(page 5)

Should poetry make intellectual demands upon us? Is it any less valuable if it presents itself in simple terms? Compare one of Blake's *Songs of Innocence* or the poetry of John Betjeman or Roger McGough with, say, one of Donne's love poems or a Shakespeare sonnet. Do you gain any more satisfaction from coming to terms with a 'difficult' poem than you do from understanding a 'straightforward' poem at first reading? Does simplicity of language necessarily go hand in hand with simplicity of meaning?

2   FRANK ... the thing is, it was an appreciation, a descriptive piece. What you have to learn is criticism.

(page 18)

Frank goes on, after this speech, to explain what he means more precisely. Read the whole passage before discussing what distinguishes literary criticism from a simple expression of what you like or don't like about a piece of writing. Is what Frank says at this point reinforced or contradicted by his reluctance to encourage Rita to change, to abandon her uniqueness later in the play (page 48)?

3   FRANK ... you seem to be under the impression that all books are literature.
      RITA Aren't they?
      FRANK No.

(page 25)

Frank has difficulty in justifying his assertion a few lines later, but his view is one that has a good deal of support among teachers and academics. What makes a piece of writing 'literature'? Why do we study some books for examination purposes and not others? Does a modern popular novel by Ian Fleming or Harold Robbins have any less to say to us than a 'classic' by Jane Austen or Charles Dickens? Do you read some books merely for light relief but others for intellectual and emotional stimulus? If so, how do you come to a decision as to which books are light and which more heavyweight? Have you ever been daunted by the prospect of reading and studying a classic by some major author, but derived immense enjoyment from the exercise once you have got into it?

4   RITA ... one line of exquisite poetry says more than a thousand pages of second-rate prose.

(page 28)

Consider this assertion. Select a single line of poetry which seems to you to contain a whole world of meaning and discuss it with other members of your group.

5   FRANK When art and literature begin to take the place of life itself, perhaps it's time to...

(page 34)

Rita interrupts him at this point, but what he is about to say is quite clear: 'perhaps it's time to abandon them.' Is it possible to give art and literature and music too central and dominant a place in our lives? What are the dangers of doing so? Is the life of every day any more real than that contained in a work of art?

6   In pairs, study carefully the discussion between Frank and Rita on the nature of tragedy (pages 40–41). Make sure you understand the main points of the argument, then improvise a parallel scene in which you use your own words to convey as clearly as you can by illustration and argument the distinction between a tragic happening and true tragedy.

91

7   RITA   ... there is not a lot of point in discussing beauti-
         ful literature in an ugly voice.

(page 56)

Is there any truth in this idea? How important is accent in
reading literature aloud? Is accent important when discussing
it? Would you be put off discussing literature with someone
like Rita who spoke coarsely and employed a lot of obscenities?

8   RITA   ... It becomes a more rewarding poem when you
         see that it works on a number of levels.

(page 61)

What does Rita mean by 'rewarding' in this context? Is it
possible to read too much into a poem or piece of prose? Do
the writer's intentions matter at all?

Education

9   FRANK   ... Most of the time, you see, it doesn't actually
          matter—appalling teaching is quite in order for most
          of my appalling students. And the others manage to
          get by despite me.

(page 13)

Do you need your teachers? Could you 'get by' without them?
Does it matter to you how they go about teaching you? Are you
worthy of them, or they of you?

10   RITA   ... You're the teacher, you sit there.

(page 15)

How do you view your teacher—as a lecturer whose every
word you take down in your notes, a repository of infinite
wisdom?—as an equal whose views on a topic are no more
nor less valid than yours?—as an enforcer of scholastic law
and order?—as an entertainer? Does it matter how the classroom furniture is arranged, who sits where?

11   FRANK   ... Proper students don't read and study.
     RITA   Y' what?
     FRANK   A joke, a joke, Yes. They read and study, some-
         times.

(page 16)

How much truth, in your experience, is there in Frank's
cynical comment? Make an honest evaluation of your own
qualities as a 'proper student'.

12   RITA   ... See, if I'd started takin' school seriously, I
         would have had to become different from me mates,
         an' that's not allowed.

(page 17)

How seriously do you and your friends take school or college?
Is it unfashionable to be too studious, to appear to want to
make progress and do well?

13   RITA   ... That's what they do wrong in schools y'
         know... they get y' talkin' an' that, an' y' all havin' a
         great time talkin' about somethin' an' the next thing
         they wanna do is turn it into a lesson.

(page 22)

Is Rita right? Do we try too hard to make lessons out of
everything in our schools? Is discussion of value in its own
right, without the drawing of conclusions or the pointing of
morals? Do teachers over-teach? Do you learn as much from
your friends and fellow students as you do from your teachers?

14   FRANK   I could have told you; but you'll have a much
         better understanding of something if you discover it in
         your own terms.

(page 31)

Is this true? Discuss its implications.

15   RITA   ... there's a time for education. An' it's not when
         y' twenty-six an' married.

(page 47)

Discuss.   93

16   RITA   Look, Frank, I don't have to go along one hundred per cent with your views on Blake y' know. I can
have a mind of my own can't I?

(page 62)

What is your relationship with those who teach you? At what
stage and to what extent can you become independent of them
and formulate views of your own? What makes the opinions
of your teachers different from yours and those of your
classmates? Are your teachers' opinions any more valid than
yours?

General

17   RITA   ... God, what's it like to be free?

(page 7)

Rita is bitter about the way in which her lifestyle (her daily
routine as a hairdresser) and her lack of formal education have
imprisoned her. In what ways does education liberate people?
Does this go for all types of education? Does a study of
literature (English or foreign) help set us free? How? Do you
feel in any sense imprisoned? What—apart from education—
might help to set you free?

18   RITA   ... if you want to change y' have to do it from the
inside, don't y'?

(page 11)

Rita is criticizing the attitude of people who think that change
in their lives is just a matter of a new hairstyle or different
clothes. How can a person be changed 'from the inside'? Is
such a change any more permanent than the sort of exterior
change Rita criticizes? Do you feel you have been changed in
this way? How did it come about?

19 RITA ... Frank, y' know culture, y' know the word culture? Well it doesn't mean goin' to the opera an' that, does it?

FRANK No.

(page 29)

What *does* 'culture' mean?

20 RITA ... It doesn't matter who's doin' it, does it? It's the same play, isn't it?

(page 38)

Is a play the same every time it is performed? Does it matter whether it is performed by amateurs or professionals? Which sort of performance do you prefer to go to? Have you ever taken part in an amateur production? What insights can we gain from acting in a play that we cannot obtain from merely reading or watching it?

21 RITA ... I can't talk to the people I live with any more.

(page 45)

What does Rita mean by this? Can education destroy our friendships and family ties? If so, what can we do about it or should we accept it as a fact of life?

Essay questions

1 What does the play gain or lose if Willy Russell's suggestion is followed and Act One, scene three is omitted?
2 Willy Russell has said that in writing *Educating Rita* he was trying to create a love story. How successful has he been in achieving his aim?
3 How far—if at all—are you able to sympathize with (a) Frank, and (b) Rita?
4 'Two lost and deluded people': is this a fair description of Frank and Rita?

STUDY QUESTIONS

5 'A simple examination of complex issues.' How far would you agree with this assessment of *Educating Rita*?

6 Is it possible to appreciate *Educating Rita* without understanding its many literary allusions?

7 Examine the suggestion that *Educating Rita* is best seen as a 1980s treatment of the old Pygmalion story.

8 'The world of *Educating Rita* is one of deep-seated and unresolved frustration.' Discuss.

9 Analyse any *one* scene of the play in order to demonstrate how Willy Russell creates his comic effects.

10 'A low comedy with a high moral purpose.' Is this how you see *Educating Rita*?